AMERICAN
IDOLS

AMERICAN

IDOLS

The WORSHIP *of the*
AMERICAN DREAM

BOB HOSTETLER

BROADMAN
& HOLMAN
PUBLISHERS

NASHVILLE, TENNESSEE

Ten-digit ISBN: 0-8054-4078-X
Thirteen digit ISBN: 978-0-8054-4078-2

Published by Broadman & Holman Publishers
Nashville, Tennessee

Dewey Decimal Classification: 261
Subject Heading: IDOLS AND IMAGES \ UNITED
STATES—SOCIAL CONDITIONS \ POPULAR
CULTURE—RELIGIOUS ASPECTS

3 4 5 6 7 8 9 10   10 09 08 07 06

Dedicated to the founders, members,
and friends of Cobblestone Community Church
in Oxford, Ohio.

Acknowledgments

Some authors write their books virtually alone, in a mountain cabin or bungalow by the sea. I don't know how that's done. I've never written a book that didn't rely on the contributions of others.

Thank you to Steve Laube of the Steve Laube Agency for representing me on this project.

Thank you to Len Goss and the folks at Broadman & Holman for believing in this book and making it better at every point in the process.

Thank you to Josh McDowell for his support and to Dave Bellis for his encouragement and mentoring over the years.

Thank you to my church family at Cobblestone Community Church, and to the leadership team for believing, not only in my pastoral ministry, but my writing ministry as well.

Thank you to the lovely Robin, my wife, who felt sorry for me at all the right times, relieved the tightness in my neck and shoulders with her loving massages, and served a vital role as sounding board and brainstormer.

"Do you love Me more than these?"

(JOHN 21:15)

Contents

Foreword by Josh McDowell   xiii

Introduction   1

1. The Oldest Competition   3
2. The eBay Attitude (Consumerism)   22
3. The Darwinian Conjecture (Naturalism)   34
4. The Cowboy Ethic (Individualism)   45
5. The Rock Star Syndrome (Celebrity)   60
6. The Microwave Mentality (Instant Gratification)   71
7. The Superman Myth (Humanism)   87
8. The Cult of Personal Experience (Experience)   102
9. The Lexus Nexus (Success)   115
10. The Eros Ethos (Sensuality, Sexual Freedom)   127
11. The Burger King Way (Choice)   144
12. The Passion for Fashion (Appearance)   154
13. The La-Z-Boy Life (Comfort)   170
14. The Modern Baal (Money)   184
15. The Martha Malady (Busyness)   205

Afterword by Matt Metzger   219

Appendix: How to Find the Church That's Right
for You   222

Notes   228

Foreword

by Josh McDowell

Seat belts are a habit in my family. When our children were small, they were secured in car seats; when they outgrew their car seats, they learned to fasten their own seat belts. I don't recall any argument or protest from them. It was just something everyone in the family did.

When my children's young friends rode in the car with us, however, they would occasionally respond indignantly when I required them to fasten their seat belts. I have had young people from the ages of three to twenty-three sigh loudly, roll their eyes at me, and act as though I were making them wear safety belts only to make them miserable.

That wasn't true, of course. I would have much preferred to have given in and saved myself the agony of their mournful cries and complaints. But I didn't. Why? Because I knew that the seat belts could save their lives. My "safety regulations" were for their own good.

If my commands to my children were for their own good, how much more do you suppose that is true of God's commands to his children? Many people react to God's laws the way young people reacted to my rules about seat belts. They see his commands as constricting. They don't see how loving and beneficial—more than that, how absolutely crucial to a successful life—God's commands are. But like the commands of a loving parent—"don't touch the stove," "look both ways before you cross the street," "eat your vegetables"—God's commands are not meant to spoil our fun and make us miserable. He didn't throw all those precepts into the Bible just because he liked the way they sounded; he didn't concoct those rules to be a killjoy or to throw his weight around; he gave those commands because he knew some things we didn't, and he wanted to protect us and provide for us.

Moses acknowledged this truth when he challenged the nation of Israel:

> And now, Israel, what does the LORD your God ask of you except to fear the LORD your God by walking in all His ways, to love Him, and to worship the LORD your God with all your heart and all your soul? Keep the LORD's commands and statutes I am giving you today *for your own good*. (Deut. 10:12–13, author's emphasis)

God issued his commands *for our good!* Looking down from an eternal, omniscient perspective, he can see things we cannot, and he issued precepts—some of them very specific—to protect us and provide for us. As Bill Hybels writes:

> The Lord tells us specifically that His commands are never burdensome (1 John 5:3). By this, He doesn't necessarily mean they're easy to keep. Rather, He's telling us that they're never foolish. They are never unnecessary or purely arbitrary. He doesn't force us to observe meaningless formalities, nor does He impose rules that have no value.
>
> On the contrary, every guideline, every law, every imperative in the Bible was crafted in infinite wisdom. They were given not only to honor God, but to benefit us as well. The entire book of Deuteronomy, for example, is a testament to this truth. In that book Moses repeatedly states that God gave the commandments for our good and promises to bless us if we obey them.[1]

This is certainly true of God's first command, given to Moses on Mount Sinai: "You shall have no other gods before me" (Exod. 20:3 NIV).

Like all the rest, that command of God was given to protect us and provide for us. God knows, even if we don't, that idolatry—in whatever form, ancient or modern, blatant or subtle—does bad things in us and to us. So he puts it right at the top of the list and has kept it there now for thousands of years. It has never moved from the number one slot!

You may think that the first command applied mainly to ancient history, back when people carved idols, erected shrines, and offered sacrifices to strange gods. Or you may believe that the first command applies today only in foreign countries or primitive cultures. You may imagine that because you live in modern times or a modern land, you don't need to give the first command a second thought.

But idolatry is not something that belongs only to the ancient past or to pagan cultures. God said, "You shall have no other gods before me" (Exod. 20:3 NIV), because he knew we would forever be tempted by other gods, strange gods, and new gods. He knew that "the human heart is most deceitful and desperately wicked" (Jer. 17:9 NLT) and prone to worship idols. He knew that—even in the twenty-first century and even (or especially) in a world that seems to be shaped increasingly by American culture—we could be led astray "with empty philosophy and high-sounding nonsense that come from human thinking and from the evil powers of this world, and not from Christ" (Col. 2:8 NLT). He knew that American idols would be no less dangerous than Canaanite, Philistine, or Babylonian idols. And he knew that as often as we succumbed to those temptations, our lives would be harder, poorer, and sadder.

God's desire is that people "will always fear me *for their own good and the good of their children after them. . . . I will rejoice in doing them good*" (Jer. 32:39, 41 NIV, author's emphasis). But our pet idolatries and cultural compromises thwart his plans, "plans to prosper you and not to harm you, plans to give you hope and a future" (Jer. 29:11 NIV). That's why I believe the message of this book is timely and important. That's why I urge you, at all costs: "Dear children, keep yourselves from idols" (1 John 5:21 NIV).

Introduction

[handwritten: assumptions ? / audience / non audience?]

You love God. You've experienced salvation through faith in Christ. You pray. You read your Bible. You worship regularly. You give financially and willingly through works of service to his kingdom.

But something is wrong. Something is missing. Something is not working. You're not alone.

There are thousands like you, in town after town, church after church, around the world. And they feel like they fall short, year after year, of their full potential as people, and especially as children of God!

Why?

[handwritten: Argument's point]

I've become convinced that often the cause is idolatry. Not so much the ancient, pagan-altar-on-a-hilltop variety, nor the light-a-candle, chant-a-mantra sort of thing, either. No, it's usually a more modern form of idolatry. More antiseptic. More American.

We seldom realize it when it happens, but our lives can easily become infected with modern idolatries that look utterly harmless, sometimes even virtuous. But these "user-friendly" idols distract us from a wholehearted, single-minded devotion to God, and become the enemies of our souls. They insert themselves between us and God. They hinder our prayers. They dull our spiritual sensitivity and impede our spiritual growth. And, like all idols, they substitute broken cisterns that hold no water for the springs of living water God wants to pour into our lives (see Jer. 2:13).

That's the reason for this book. If we systematically and carefully examine ourselves for the purpose of preventing or rooting out the most dangerous and tenacious idols of today, we may not only preserve our effectiveness but invite even greater blessing on our lives. We may come to know the one true God to be an extent we've not yet experienced or even imagined.

That's my prayer for you as you read.

ONE

The Oldest Competition

I t started quietly enough in the summer of 2002. Three talent scouts named Randy, Paula, and Simon traveled to several American cities to find the next "American Idol." In each city they auditioned hundreds of potential singing idols, but only thirty at each site moved on to the next round of competition.

Unlike previous television successes, like *Ted Mack's Original Amateur Hour* and *Star Search*, the Fox network's *American Idol* grabbed viewers not only with some fine performers but also with some agonizingly atrocious moments, like Keith's third-season rendition of the Madonna hit, "Like a Virgin." Some of those atrocious moments were funny enough or charming enough to vault the performer—or perpetrator—to fame and fortune. For example, William Hung's rendition of Ricky Martin's "She Bangs" netted him a recording contract, a fan club, a commercial, a movie role, guest appearances on *Ellen* and *The George Lopez Show*, and his very own bobble-head doll!

So far the winners of the *American Idol* competition have all ascended to the stardom they were promised. First-season winner Kelly Clarkson and runner-up Justin Guarini released records and costarred in a movie (Clarkson's debut single became the fastest chart-climber in history). Second season winner Ruben Studdard and runner-up Clay Aiken enjoyed even greater success; Aiken's debut single, "This Is the Night," reached number one on the Billboard Hot 100 chart in its first week—only the twelfth song in history to do that. And Fantasia Barrino, the winner of *Idol*'s third season, duplicated Aiken's feat with her single, "I Believe."

The series has weathered controversy and scandal to become one of the hottest shows on television, most recently auditioning over one hundred thousand "idol wannabes" in seven different cities. Its fourth season debuted with 33.5 million viewers, more than ever before. Its contestants become instant icons. Each new round makes news. And yet American idols are nothing new.

America has long been rife with idols, but not the Fantasia Barrino or Clay Aiken kind. The idols we worship are far more numerous than the contestants who make it to Hollywood and the final few episodes of *American Idol*. They are real. They are dangerous. And chances are, they are affecting your life—and that of your family, friends, and church—to a shocking degree.

America: An Idol-Free Zone?

We don't think of ourselves as idolaters. The idea seems absurd. Sure, we idolize athletes and movie stars, but that's a different category altogether. We don't really traffic in idols. That stuff is all so ancient—as in ancient Greece, ancient Rome, ancient Bithynia. Those people worshipped idols, but not us. We're too modern for that.

We're also too American for idol worship. We know there are people in other parts of the world who bow to idols. We've seen the photos in *National Geographic* of Buddha statues surrounded by flowers, candles, and incense left by devotees. We've heard of people in other cultures keeping handmade gods in their huts. The worship of idols is something that belongs, if not to another age, certainly to a much different culture. Right?

Not so fast. It is true, as author Elyse Fitzpatrick says, that "America doesn't have idols on every corner and days set aside to burn incense or light lanterns to our gods. We don't have large temples where we offer bowls of rice [to a god]. . . . In fact, 76 percent of Americans polled 'consider themselves completely true to the First Commandment,' 'You shall have no other gods before Me' (Exod. 20:3 NIV)."[1] We don't keep a golden calf in our garden or chant prayers to an image. But that doesn't necessarily mean that our lives are free of idols. It may just mean that our idols are more subtle. It may mean that the idols we worship, we "worship in ignorance," like the ancient Athenians (Acts 17:23). It may mean that we have "refined idolatry to make it a part of everyday life," as journalist and former missionary Marshall Allen suggests.[2]

You see, generally speaking, none of us fall into idolatrous beliefs and behaviors intentionally—at least not at first. We don't set out to succumb to idolatry. We don't aspire to become idolaters. It's a subtle process, sinister even, imperceptible at first. It's a slow process, one that can take months or years to bud. It's a gradual process, starting out as a seedling but eventually growing stubborn and strong.

But it is also a fairly predictable process, as the experience of the Hebrews in the wilderness sets out for us.

Idolatry 101

In some ways the Israelite camp of 1500 BC may not have been so different from twenty-first-century America, and their spiritual longings—and choices—may be more similar than we imagine:

Zimri patted his stomach and leaned back on the soft pillows his wife had brought from Egypt. "It is a happy man whose wife cooks like that," he said.

His wife, Zebidah, smiled demurely and spoke without looking at her husband. "Will you join the delegation?"

He frowned. "It's not an uprising. It's nothing like that."

She nodded and wiped a bead of perspiration from her temple. The heat inside the tent would soon become insufferable, as it did every day in this desert wasteland.

"No one expected Moses to be gone this long," he said. "We just need a plan, that's all." He sensed sadness in his wife, disapproval, perhaps.

"I'm sure you are wise," she said.

Zimri felt his anger rise. He hated it when she said things like that. She was a strong woman and a smart one, and he often felt that she knew more than she spoke and understood more than he. Well, this time it was she who did not understand.

He rose suddenly from the floor and ducked through the open flaps of the tent. He looked one way and then the other and finally spied Shlomo leading a group of twenty or thirty men. They were coming in his direction.

"Come!" Shlomo shouted, crooking an arm around Zimri's neck. "We go to Aaron's tent!"

Zimri had no choice but to fall in step with Shlomo, at the head of the delegation. A bearded face appeared between his head and Shlomo's.

"Zimri son of Eli, I have heard you speak," the man said. "You speak well."

"He is right, you know," Shlomo said. "You should speak for us."

"No!" Zimri said. "Not me. I wouldn't know what to say."

"What is there to know? You tell Aaron what we talked about around the fire. You tell him to lead or get out of the way."

"But I—" The delegation was already at the tent of Aaron the priest, the brother of Moses. Shlomo and the other man pushed him forward just as Aaron stepped through the flaps. Zimri turned to protest to Shlomo and saw with horror that the crowd behind him had grown. Hundreds of men and women stood behind him!

Zimri turned back to face Aaron. The priest said nothing, apparently content to wait. Zimri cast one more pleading look at Shlomo but saw nothing but determination in his expression.

He cleared his throat. "Your brother Moses," he started, casting a glance at the mountain Moses had entered weeks ago. The apex was shrouded in dark clouds that intermittently emanated rumblings and flashings that frightened everyone below. "He has not returned."

Aaron did not respond.

Zimri licked his lips. "It has been weeks."

Still no response. "The camp is restless. Fearful. The children especially."

Aaron's gaze left Zimri's face and traveled behind him as if searching the faces of the others.

Zimri cleared his throat again. "Our progress has halted. There is no word from the mountain." He felt his courage gathering inside him now. "There is no indication of when we will move from this ominous place. It is not good for our spirits. It is not good for our families. It is not good for the nation."

He cast a glance behind him and saw several heads nodding. His words seemed to be finding a home in their hearts and minds.

"You are a priest to us," he appealed to Aaron. "And we have been instructed to come to you in Moses' absence. So we come."

Aaron still had not spoken. Zimri felt his emotional temperature rising. "Come!" he said, his voice now strong, stentorian. "Make us gods who will go before us, who will unite us, who will get us moving again. Is

this not what we came here for? Not to die in the
desert, not to be consumed in the mountain, but to
become a great and mighty nation for the glory of our
gods!"

He was almost done. He could feel the energy of
the crowd behind him, urging him forward, like the
swell of a mighty sea. "As for this Moses, the one who
brought us up out of Egypt," he said, lifting his gaze
once more up the slope of the dark mountain, and then
slowly turning it back to Aaron, "we don't know what
has happened to him."

Suddenly, voices rose behind Zimri, agreeing with
him and protesting Aaron's inaction.

Zimri saw the priest shoot an angry look at him
before lifting his chin so his voice would carry far.
"Consider the cost, for it will be high," Aaron said.
"Take off the gold earrings you are wearing—and your
wives, your sons, and your daughters—and bring every
single one of them to me."

Zimri's lips tightened into a thin line. He saw
immediately what Aaron was doing. He was demanding
the people's recent plunder from Egypt, the earrings
that the Egyptians had virtually thrown at their escaping
slaves. They would not so soon part with such new
treasure.

Shlomo was the first. He shouldered his way past
Zimri and made a show of placing a large gold earring
before Aaron's sandaled feet. It took a moment, but
others soon followed, and before long people were
running back to their tents for more gold.

Zimri saw the priest's face tighten. The bluff had
not worked. A pile of gold jewelry lay in the dust
between Aaron and Zimri.

Within days a golden calf had been fashioned from
the people's offerings, and Zimri stood proudly at the
foot of the mountain while the image was erected.
"These," he shouted, "are your gods, O Israel, who
brought you up out of Egypt." The people cheered, and
Zimri watched as Aaron came forward and placed a large

stone in front of the calf, indicating where the altar would soon be built.

"Tomorrow," Aaron announced, to more cheers, "there will be a festival to the Lord."

Music and dancing broke out spontaneously as Zimri made his way through the crowd and found his wife Zebidah. He searched her eyes for some sign of approval but found none. He sighed. "It is a festival to the Lord," he said. "You heard what Aaron said."

They walked in silence for a few moments. Zimri hated it that he felt the need to defend himself to a woman. "The people cannot worship a god they cannot see," he explained. "The calf is merely an aid to worship, an aid to faith. It gives the people something to unite around, something to feel good about. You see that, don't you?"

"I'm sure you are wise," she said.

The Alchemy of Idolatry

That scene, of course, is largely out of my imagination. But it's based on the biblical record of Exodus 32, which records the Israelites' impatience with Moses' sojourn on Mt. Sinai and their subsequent appeal to Aaron to "make us an image of a god who will lead and protect us" (Exod. 32:1 CEV).

The experience of Israel in the wilderness is not so far removed from us. What happened when Moses was on the mountain (and his brother Aaron was trying to keep it together in the valley) is a depiction of our own tendencies, weaknesses, and idolatries.

In fact, though the writer's intention was simply to record what happened there at the foot of Mt. Sinai, not to give us a recipe for idolatry, we can still find seven ingredients in that Exodus account that may lead us to a better understanding of our own idolatrous tendencies. In just seven short verses (Exod. 32:1–7), we can identify a basic formula for the creation and cultivation of an idol.

Impatience

The account of Israel's idolatry begins:

> When the people saw that Moses was so long in coming
> down from the mountain, they gathered around Aaron.
> (Exod. 32:1a NIV)

Moses had apparently given the Israelites no indication of how
long he would be with God on Mt. Sinai; he was simply following
God a day at a time, it seems.

Meanwhile, back at the ranch, folks got impatient. The biblical account doesn't say whether they approached Aaron after a
week, a few weeks, or more; but it's clear that Moses had been on
the mountain with God long enough for them to wonder if he
was still alive in that stark, unforgiving environment.

Impatience is an ingredient of idolatry, in all of its forms.
Elyse Fitzpatrick, in her book *Idols of the Heart* writes:

> In the middle of this instant, *Give it to me quickly! It*
> *better be convenient!* culture, we tend to think that God
> should work in our lives in the same way. . . . *Quickly,*
> *Lord, if you don't mind.*[3]

We turn to idols because we refuse to wait for God's timing,
for his answers, for his provision. We seek satisfaction from ille-
gitimate sources because we don't want to wait for satisfaction
from our legitimate Source.

Unbelief

The next thing we see about the Israelites' experience at Sinai is
how their slide into idolatry was fueled by ignorance and unbelief.

> "This Moses, the man who brought us up from the land
> of Egypt—*we don't know* what has happened to him!"
> (Exod. 32:1 NIV, author's emphasis)

Now, it's possible that the delegation's words to Aaron were
merely a dodge; they may have been pushing their agenda aside
from any concern for Moses.

But what if something *had* happened to Moses? What if they waited another month? Two months? How long could they remain in the barrenness of Sinai without their leader, their deliverer? Who can blame them?

It's not hard to believe that the people urged Aaron to give them an idol because they honestly didn't know what had become of Moses. They didn't know what would happen next. They didn't know what the future held. And that uncertainty presented them with a choice: faith or unbelief.

To continue to wait would have had to have been an act of faith, not in Moses, but in God. It would have meant believing that, even if Moses had died of a heart attack up there in all the smoke and thunder, God could still lead them, still provide for them, still deliver them.

But that is a lot to ask of finite human beings not only in Israel's day but in ours, too. None of us can see into the future. *We don't know* what will happen tomorrow. We don't know whether our prayers will be answered as we hope and expect. We don't know just what troubles—or blessings—wait around the next corner. And that daily uncertainty presents us with a daily choice: faith or unbelief. We choose faith when we trust God's love and his willingness to make sure "that every detail in our lives . . . is worked into something good" (Rom. 8:28 *The Message*). We choose unbelief when we, like Rebekah and Jacob (see Gen. 27), try to acquire with our own scheming and straining what we're afraid God will not provide for us.

Pragmatism

With impatience and unbelief, another ingredient of idolatry is something we might call pragmatism: "They gathered around Aaron and said to him, 'Come, make us a god who will go before us'" (Exod. 32:1 NIV).

It seems so shocking to us, so blatant, to hear God's people say those words. We would never say such a thing, at least not in so many words. Yet it made perfect sense to their minds, as it will

In our image

to ours once we grasp what they were really asking: they wanted a god they could see, a god who could lead them, a god they could rally around, a god who was a little more like them.

That is so often the case with us in the idols we craft for ourselves. We tend to fashion gods after our own image instead of allowing God to fashion us after his image. As Elyse Fizpatrick writes:

> Idolatry is a sin that has its beginning in the mind, in your thoughts, beliefs, judgments, and imagination. Asaph rebuked the Israelites because they had created a god in their own image: "you thought that I was just like you" (Ps. 50:21 NASB). Incorrect thinking about God's character breeds idolatry. . . . If we imagine a god who exists to pander to our fickle desires or who gives up in frustration because he can't accomplish his will, we're worshiping a false god.[4]

Our idols, you see, are not smelted from jewelry or fashioned from clay like the BC brand of idolatry. We tend to create practical idols, idols that have the feel of the familiar to us, idols that don't demand so much from us. Our pet idolatries are mostly those that help us blend in better with our culture, that make us more comfortable in twenty-first-century America. Our American idols are often dressed in the clothes of practicality and convenience, of assimilation and acceptance.

It's all very sensible. Easy. User-friendly. A crucial ingredient for a serviceable idol.

Ingratitude

Another element we find in the boiling cauldron of idolatry is ingratitude for God's actions and purposes in our lives. It's striking that the mob referred to Moses as "this fellow" who brought them out of Egypt, as if he were a hired hand or a gate-crasher. It's amazing how they can admit that Moses was instrumental in their deliverance from slavery . . . and yet in the next breath propose more or less giving the guy up for dead!

More significant, though, is the fact that there is no mention of their Divine Deliverer in their speech to Aaron. How many times had they heard:

> "Remember this day when you came out of Egypt, out of the place of slavery, for the LORD brought you out of here by the strength of [His] hand." (Exod. 13:3)
>
> "On that day explain to your son, 'This is because of what the LORD did for me when I came out of Egypt.'" (Exod. 13:8)
>
> "This evening you will know that it was the LORD who brought you out of the land of Egypt." (Exod. 16:6)

They had been delivered from an oppressive and painful slavery. They had seen mind-boggling miracles. They had been guided by a pillar of fire and a column of cloud. They had vowed to obey everything God had said to them (Exod. 19:8). Yet, "although they knew God, they neither glorified him as God nor gave thanks to him" (Rom. 1:21 NIV).

When you and I neglect the habit of worship, both corporate and private, we open the door to idolatry. When prayers of thanksgiving slow to a trickle, or stop, we make ourselves vulnerable. When we forget God's actions and purposes to such a degree that we neither glorify him nor give thanks to him, we should beware. Such ingratitude is a catalyst for the creation of an idol.

Regression

What began as spiritual impatience in the Israelite camp led to spiritual regression.

Aaron's choice of a golden calf as the golden image for Israel to worship was not accidental or random. While the Egyptians worshipped many gods that were depicted in animal form—such as frogs, crocodiles, flies, and fish—one of the most important was Apis, the bull god of Memphis, who came to be associated with Ptah, the creator of the universe.

Aaron and his people clearly reassured themselves that nothing was amiss. This was not Apis they were molding; it was representative, not of the gods of Egypt, but of the gods who brought them *out of* Egypt. But in creating a golden calf, the Israelites were nonetheless reverting to the familiar, the comfortable, the easy.

Such regression is common to the heart that is prone to idolatry. Spiritual growth slows, then stops. Victory over temptation increasingly becomes a thing of the past. Former faults and frailties seem to return, often with a vengeance. And often, like the Israelites, the heart that is slipping into idolatry is none the wiser, perhaps because it all has the feel of the familiar to it.

Compromise

Aaron is such a fascinating character in the drama of Exodus 32. At times he seems to agree with the Israelites' demands and proclamations; at other times he seems to be trying to adapt, to channel their efforts into less destructive courses.

He fashions the calf, but then seems to step back from the forefront:

> He took what they handed him and made it into an idol cast in the shape of a calf, fashioning it with a tool. Then they said, "These are your gods, O Israel, who brought you up out of Egypt."
> When Aaron saw this, he built an altar in front of the calf and announced, "Tomorrow there will be a festival to the LORD." (Exod. 32:4–5 NIV)

It's not hard to see what Aaron was trying to do. He was saying, in effect, "OK, if you must have an idol, let's at least call it the Lord. Let's not abandon the first commandment, even if you insist on breaking the second."

It was a ridiculous compromise. Surely they knew this bull was not the God who brought them out of Egypt. Surely they could see that this quadruped was the image of a creature, not the Creator. Surely they recognized that this was "an idol cast from metal," an "image of a bull, which eats grass" (Ps. 106:19–20 NIV). They knew, but they rationalized: "Tomorrow there will be a festival to the LORD" (Exod. 32:5 NIV).

Such compromise is an important part of the recipe. Idolatry is seldom outright, defiant rejection of the one, true God. Few of us allow our idols to totally displace God in our affections and allegiances. We, like Aaron and the Israelites, more often reach a compromise: God *as*, God *and*, God *with*, or God *alongside*.

Corruption

Like the layer of grease that rises from a pan of gravy, corruption will rise from the cauldron of idolatry, both an ingredient and a product. After Aaron proclaimed a festival to the Lord:

> The next day the people rose early and sacrificed burnt offerings and presented fellowship offerings. Afterward they sat down to eat and drink and got up to indulge in revelry. (Exod. 32:6 NIV)

what did they do before

You might say their worship combined the best of both worlds, from one viewpoint. They presented offerings to the Lord and enjoyed food and drink, which were legitimate features of Yahweh worship. And they indulged in excess and revelry, which were characteristic of the ways Egyptians celebrated their feast of Apis.

But, of course, corrupted worship of the one, true God is not worship of him at all. You cannot mix Living Water and sewage into a potable blend. You cannot make dance partners of holiness and idolatry.

As God informed Moses on the mountain:

> "Your people, whom you brought up out of Egypt, have become corrupt. They have been quick to turn away from what I commanded them." (Exod. 32:7–8 NIV)

When God says they "have become corrupt," he uses a word (*shahat*) which also means "devastated," "ruined." It is the same word the Bible uses to refer to the condition of the earth that provoked the flood (Gen. 6:12). Such corruption is the result of idolatry—both ancient and modern.

When you and I create idols out of our impatience, unbelief, pragmatism, ingratitude, regression, and compromise, corruption will invariably bubble up and spew forth. Our walk with God will be corrupted. Our worship will be corrupted. Our service, our relationships, and our testimony will all become corrupted.

"Look What I Found!"

Moses was warned by God on the mount that his people had "become corrupt" and "been quick to turn away" from the commands of God. When he arrived at the scene of the crime, the Bible says Moses confronted his brother Aaron:

> He said to Aaron, "What did these people do to you, that you led them into such great sin?"
>
> "Do not be angry, my lord," Aaron answered. "You know how prone these people are to evil. They said to me, 'Make us gods who will go before us. As for this fellow Moses who brought us up out of Egypt, we don't know what has happened to him.' So I told them, 'Whoever has any gold jewelry, take it off.' Then they gave me the gold, and I threw it into the fire, and out came this calf!" (Exod. 32:21–24 NIV)

Sure, Aaron's response sounds ridiculous. But the fact of the matter is, whenever you or I mix together impatience, unbelief, pragmatism, ingratitude, regression, compromise, and corruption, we too may be surprised at what idols emerge!

Name Your God

Idolatry is not passé. It is as current as impatience and unbelief. It is as modern as pragmatism, ingratitude, and regression. It is as up-to-date as compromise and corruption.

Nor does idolatry belong only in the pagan world where unbelievers bow to superstition and foreigners practice strange rituals. No, idolatry is at home in our own culture, and even in our churches. As John Calvin said, "Man's nature . . . is a perpetual factory of idols."[5]

So what are the idols we worship? Not Apis or Baal. Not Dagon, whom the Philistines worshipped, or Marduk, the false god of the Babylonians. Our idols are of a different sort entirely, but they are no less real and no less dangerous. They are idols like consumerism and individualism. Or choice and comfort. Or appearance and experience. Not that there's anything inherently wrong with all those things, just as there was nothing sinful about the Israelites' golden earrings. But just as Aaron made their gold into an idol, we can make such things as success and sexuality into an idol.

Our American idols may be harder to recognize than the worship of a stone idol. They may also be harder to correct. But they are attitudes and lifestyles that are abominations to God, and if we don't do something about them, they will corrupt and devastate us just as they did the Israelites in the wilderness of Sinai.

No Idols Here?

The purpose of this book is to help you recognize and overcome the idols you worship. "But," you may say, "I'm not aware of any idols in my life." Or, "Sure, I could be a little more focused on God in this area or that area, but that doesn't mean I'm an idolater, for crying out loud." You may even say, like Peter, "Maybe others, but not me" (see Matt. 26:33). *LOL*

Fair enough. But suppose—just suppose—there is something standing between you and God, something hindering answers to your most heartfelt prayers, something impeding your spiritual growth, something making it hard for you to feel God's presence and experience his blessing on your life. Suppose you could discover

the reason for your lack of victory over some habitual sin or your
lack of deliverance from some burden or bitterness. Suppose, as
Oswald Chambers wrote, your eyes have been blinded "in this your
day [to] the things that make for your peace" (Luke 19:42 NKJV):

> [On the first Palm Sunday,] Jesus entered Jerusalem tri-
> umphantly and the city was stirred to its very founda-
> tions, but a strange god was there—the pride of the
> Pharisees. It was a god that seemed religious and
> upright, but Jesus compared it to "whitewashed tombs
> which indeed appear beautiful outwardly, but inside
> are full of dead men's bones and all uncleanness"
> (Matt. 23:27 NKJV).
>   What is it that blinds you to the peace of God "in
> this *your* day"? Do you have a strange god—not a dis-
> gusting monster but perhaps an unholy nature that con-
> trols your life? More than once God has brought me
> face to face with a strange god in my life, and I knew
> that I should have given it up, but I didn't do it. I got
> through the crisis "by the skin of my teeth," only to find
> myself still under the control of that strange god.
> I am blind to the very things that make for my own
> peace. It is a shocking thing that we can be in the exact
> place where the Spirit of God should be having His
> completely unhindered way with us, and yet we only
> make matters worse, increasing our blame in God's
> eyes.[6]

Are you willing to explore whether you may have a strange
god—not a disgusting monster but perhaps an unholy nature—
that corrupts your worship or controls your life? Or impedes your
prayers? Or disturbs your peace?

How to Use This Book

Each of the chapters that follow will focus on one of more
than a dozen typically American idols we tend to worship not only
as individuals but sometimes even as churches. It's unlikely that

nay sayghs

you will find yourself prone to all, or even most, of them. But it should not surprise you if God uses these chapters to bring you face-to-face with more than one strange god in your life. When he does, your response will be crucial. *what I want u*
2 ous with the info.

Recognize

As you read, please resist the urge to rationalize or make excuses, as Aaron did (Exod. 32:22–24). Let your response be more like that of Moses:

> When Moses approached the camp and saw the calf and the dancing, his anger burned and he threw the tablets out of his hands, breaking them to pieces at the foot of the mountain. (Exod. 32:19 NIV)

This response was no temper tantrum. No, in that time and culture, when a person or nation broke a tablet, it meant the cancellation of a contract. Moses was emphasizing to his people that they had effectively broken their contract with God, their vow to obey everything God had said to them (Exod. 19:8). By breaking the tablets, Moses helped the Israelites confront the severity of their sin.

So, too, when we recognize an idol in our lives, we must face it squarely. In fact, you should be encouraged when God shows you the idols you worship because the more idols you recognize and overcome as you read this book, the more liberating and exhilarating your subsequent spiritual progress is likely to be. But *2 parts* recognizing your idols is only half the battle; you must also take steps to overcome them.

Repent

How do we begin the steps of casting down our idols? "We start," writes Marshall Allen, "by calling [idolatry] what it is—sin. Then we confess it to God and ask Him to forgive us and continue revealing our sin to us as our faith matures."[7]

Those are crucial first steps. But since many of our idolatries are ingrained in our beliefs and behaviors, we will need to go beyond those first steps and find ways to cultivate new beliefs and try new behaviors until we have succeeded in taking off the old and putting on the new, as the Bible puts it (see Eph. 4:22–24).

Exercise

When Moses returned to the Israelite camp, he not only emphasized the seriousness of their sin by breaking the tablets of the covenant; the Bible says he did something else:

> Then he took the calf they had made, burned it up, and ground it to powder. He scattered the powder over the surface of the water and forced the Israelites to drink it. (Exod. 32:20)

We might call this action an object lesson or a "spiritual formation exercise." Apparently it was not enough to destroy the idol and stop its worship; Moses required the Israelites to perform an action, one that was probably intended to guide their future behavior and be remembered for a long time.

Similarly, each chapter in this book will include a suggested "spiritual formation" assignment. If you're not familiar with the term *spiritual formation*, don't worry; it simply refers to the practice of taking a purposeful approach to spiritual growth, undertaking new exercises or disciplines in order to develop new spiritual muscles, so to speak.

When a chapter helps you to recognize and repent of an idol in your life—or something in danger of becoming an idol—please consider adopting or adapting the spiritual formation assignment. As with physical exercise, of course, you should not expect to perform the exercise once and be done with it. Instead, prayerfully repeat the exercise—even after you go on to read subsequent chapters and adopt subsequent exercises—until you develop a strong sense that the idol has been cast down. Even then, however, your work may not be done; you may periodically want to repeat that particular exercise to keep your "spiritual muscles" strong and prevent a relapse.

Don't think you need to undertake this practice and cast down your idols all by yourself. Enlisting a partner—or a small group—to study these chapters with you can greatly enhance your experience and speed your progress. You can even find group study notes for every chapter in this book, free of charge, by going to www.bobhostetler.com and clicking on the *American Idols* link.   *did you?*

Pray

Finally, each chapter will conclude with a prayer. Even after breaking the tablets, making the Israelites drink the dregs of their own idolatry, and ruthlessly purging the camp of the unrepentant ringleaders (Exod. 32:25–29), the process was incomplete until Moses prayed (Exod. 32:31–32). Similarly, our efforts to recognize and overcome the idols we worship will be worthless and ineffectual until we pray. You may pray silently or aloud. You may pray the exact words printed on the page or adapt them to reflect more closely the desires of your heart. You may copy them into your personal prayer journal. You may pray them once or several times daily for a certain length of time. But please do not neglect the prayers because the process will be woefully incomplete without prayer.

Just a few chapters from now, you may be climbing to new spiritual heights and enjoying new levels of effectiveness as your heart begins to sing—and your life begins to reflect—the prayer of the hymn writer:

> *The dearest idol I have known,*
> *Whate'er that idol be,*
> *Help me to tear it from thy throne,*
> *And worship only thee.*
> —William Cowper, 1772

The eBay Attitude

EBay is a true twenty-first-century phenomenon. From 1995 to 1998, eBay did no outside advertising, yet it grew from 289,000 items for sale in 1996 to over thirteen million today, with registered users numbering over 135 million.[1]

In fact, there are more than eighteen thousand *categories* of items to buy on eBay:

> antiques and art,
> books, CDs, movies, coins,
> clothing,
> crafts,
> dolls,
> electronics,
> jewelry,
> stamps,
> home furnishings,
> pottery and glass,

tickets, toys, musical instruments,
cars, motorcycles, and who knows what else?
You can buy on eBay all kinds of stuff you need and even
more stuff you don't need. Like a 1970s mint-condition *Six
Million Dollar Man* action figure, five hundred dollars' worth
of Lee Majors. Or an original Van Gogh painting for half a million dollars. Or a "36-inch nonslip Pimple Grip Dressage Whip"
(which is an oddly poetic term for a horse whip).

And, while eBay is a worldwide phenomenon, it is also a
typically, quintessentially American idol. *?*

The Desire to Acquire

EBay is just one example of an epidemic of desire in our culture and even in the church: the desire to acquire. Journalist and
former missionary Marshall Allen writes:

> In Nairobi, Kenya, hundreds of thousands of people
> live in disease-ridden slums consisting of shacks cobbled
> together from wood scraps and plastic wrap. These
> shanties are propped against one another upon acres of
> dust, which becomes mud when it rains. Open trenches,
> where human excrement floats in stagnant water,
> crisscross the terrain. . . .
> The poverty and suffering in Kenya and in other
> parts of the Third World are striking to American
> visitors. But . . . Kenyans exhibit a love for one another
> and a zest for life that's [enviable]. It's almost become
> cliché for American Christians to return from trips to
> the Third World, saying in amazement: The people are
> so poor, they have nothing—and yet they have such joy,
> they seem so happy!
> This stock phrase reveals more about the United
> States—and Christianity in America—than it does about
> poor people in the Third World. It exposes a Godless
> assumption.[2]

That godless assumption is at the root of our eBay attitude. It is what motivates me to spend myself into debt. It is what prompts me never to be satisfied with what I have. It is what causes me to keep wanting more and more. It is one of several assumptions that our culture believes and teaches until they become articles of faith, even in us who worship God and follow Jesus. The first of these godless assumptions can be stated as "having more things will make me happier."

Having More Will Make Me Happier

"You CAN buy happiness," boasts an ad for a shopping mall, "just don't pay retail."

Many advertisers on television and in magazines are not selling products, primarily; they're selling happiness. The right car, the right jewelry, the right shampoo, the right bathroom fixtures, and *voila!* you can be as happy as the gorgeous models in the ad.

The fact is, things *can* bring happiness. Yup. You read that right. Things *can* bring happiness. Things can make you happy. If you get a gift—especially one that is chosen well—you feel happy. The problem is: it's temporary. After a while the thrill is gone. The excitement fades. Boredom sets in.

Were you thrilled over last year's Christmas gift? Are you still? Last year's birthday gift? Can you even remember it?

King Solomon once said:

> He who loves money shall never have enough. The foolishness of thinking that wealth brings happiness! The more you have, the more you spend. (Eccl. 5:10–11 TLB)

Humorist and author Phil Callaway said: "Having enough is nowhere near as much fun as I thought it was going to be when I didn't have any."

How many of us used to *dream* of the day when we would earn the kind of money we're earning now? And how many of us have found that to be enough?

Uh-huh. That's what I'm saying.

Dr. Herbert Schlossberg, author of *Idols for Destruction,* writes:

> All true needs—such as food, drink, and companion-
> ship—are satiable. Illegitimate wants—pride, envy,
> greed—are insatiable. By their nature they cannot be
> satisfied. In that sense materialism is the opiate of the
> people. Enough is never enough.[3]

Wow!

In fact, not only is the acquisition of more things unlikely to satisfy us and make us happier; there is evidence that it could actually make us less happy. "The subversive paradox of materialism," says Marshall Allen, "is that it might be a primary cause of unhappiness." He cites Barry Schwartz, a professor at Swarthmore College in Pennsylvania:

> Schwartz wrote . . . that the American "happiness quo-
> tient" has consistently declined for more than a genera-
> tion. "In the last 30 years—a time of great prosperity—
> the proportion of the population describing itself as
> 'very happy' has declined," Schwartz wrote. The decline
> was about 5 percent, which translates into 14 million
> Americans. Schwartz said the "happiness quotient" has
> decreased because of an abundance of choices and a
> consumer attitude that pervades our lives.[4]

Having more things will not make us happier. It could even make us feel worse. But that's not the only godless assumption at the root of our idolatry. Another is the belief that having more things will make us more important.

Having More Will Make Me More Important

In the delightful musical play *Fiddler on the Roof,* the main character is a poor milkman named Tevye. Overworked and underpaid, he tells God, "I realize that it's no great shame to be poor; but it's no great honor, either. So would it have been so terrible if I had a small fortune?" He goes on to sing, "If I Were a Rich Man," fantasizing that:

The most important men in town would come to fawn on
me!
They would ask me to advise them. . . .
And it won't make one bit of difference if I answer right
or wrong.
When you're rich, they think you really know!

We equate our net worth with our self-worth. We think that
people who own more than we do are more important than we
are. Conversely, we believe that those who own little count for
little. So we buy things we don't need with money we don't have
to impress people we don't even like!

Having more things does not make us more important.
A no-less-important man than Jesus once said:

Be on your guard against greed in any shape or form.
For a man's real life in no way depends on the number
of his possessions. (Luke 12:15 *Phillips*)

We think that having more things will make us more
important. But, of course, it doesn't.

Having More Things Will Make Me More Secure

I'll confess, I am highly prone to this form of idolatry. And
then I remember Donald Trump. He'll always be a lot richer than
I am, but in the late 1980s he lost millions of dollars in a short
time. I take no small amount of comfort in the awareness that,
no matter what happens, I will never lose anywhere near that
much money!

Howard Hughes didn't become more secure as he became
more wealthy. In fact, he became so fearful and insecure that
he died a lonely, pathetic recluse who couldn't trust anyone or
anything.

The Bible says: "The rich man thinks of his wealth as an
impregnable defense, a high wall of safety. What a dreamer!"
(Prov. 18:11 TLB).

"The sleep of the worker is sweet," said Solomon, "whether he eats little or much; but the abundance of the rich permits him *loe* no sleep" (Eccl. 5:12). He lamented the accumulation of wealth as a "grievous evil," pointing out:

> I have seen a grievous evil under the sun:
> wealth hoarded to the harm of its owner,
>   or wealth lost through some misfortune,
> so that when he has a son
>   there is nothing left for him.
> Naked a man comes from his mother's womb,
>   and as he comes, so he departs.
> (Eccl. 5:13–15 NIV)

In other words, the more material wealth you have, the more harm you're exposed to—perhaps even becoming someone you wouldn't want to become. The more you have, the more you stand to lose. The more you have, the more it takes to maintain it. The more you have, the more you have to pay to insure it. And you can take none of it with you when you die. *My car — no lock*

The truth is, real security can only be found when you place your trust in something that can't be taken away from you. If you put your security in things, you have a false security because things can be taken from you a million different ways—legally or illegally.

Thousands of years ago, a man who knew what it was to be rich and knew what it was to lose it all said:

> If I put my trust in money, if my happiness depends on
> wealth, . . . it would mean that I have denied the God
> of heaven. (Job 31:24–25, 28 TLB)

Why did he say that? Because whatever you trust in for your security is your god. People of the ancient world placed their trust in stone carvings or clay statues to secure them against rain, flood, famine, disease, infertility, and so on. They put their hope in Baal or Ashtaroth to try to lessen the odds that they would have the cosmic rug pulled out from under them.

We, however, are much more sophisticated than that. We trust our employer, our insurer, our bank account, our 401K, our portfolio, our possessions for security. None of those things is bad, mind you. But to whatever degree we trust them for security, we are treating them as idols. Rather than bowing before the true God and saying, "Our help is in the Lord, the maker of heaven and earth" (Ps. 124:8), we're placing our hope, our faith, our trust in things because we think having more things will make us happier, more important, or more secure. But we know that's just not true.

Rethinking the eBay Attitude

OK, sure, that all sounds good, but is it really possible to transform our eBay attitude? Is it even reasonable to think we can live in a consumer-driven culture without bowing down to it, without giving in to it, without prostituting ourselves at the altar of consumerism?

I'll suggest, as briefly as possible, four steps, each of which is drawn straight out of the pages of the Bible.

Repent

There's only one way to correct idolatry, and that is simply and completely to repent of it. The prophet Hosea appealed to his people:

> Return to the LORD and say,
> "Please forgive our sins. . . .
> We will no longer worship
> the idols we have made." (Hos. 14:2–3 CEV)

To which God answered:

> "I will heal you of your idolatry and faithlessness, and
> my love will know no bounds." (Hos. 14:4 NLT)

So the first step in overthrowing the idol of consumerism is to get honest. Ask God to reveal to you the depths of your idolatry and faithlessness so he can heal you.

Former missionary Marshall Allen tells of an experience when he lived in Kenya:

> One time, I cleaned out my closet to rid myself of my old flip-flops, faded shorts and T-shirts. I gave the clothing to a missionary friend so he could deliver it as an anonymous gift to some of our Kenyan friends. About a week later, I attended a Bible study with a group of the same Kenyans. Three of the guys in attendance were proudly outfitted in my cast-off clothing. As I saw how pleased they were to have "new" clothes, I was suddenly startled. Then I felt ashamed. I had known their need, but only gave my unwanted clothing to make room in my closet for newer clothes. Materialism motivated even my generosity.[5]

Confess your idolatry and repent of it before God. Be as specific as you can, recalling the purchases you've made and the things you have amassed. Admit to God that you put faith in those material things, hoping they would make you happier, more important, and more secure.

"Take words with you," as Hosea pleaded, "and return to the LORD. Say to him: 'Forgive all [my] sins and receive [me] graciously'" (Hos. 14:2 NIV). That is the first step. But repentance will involve more than words.

Resist

Arthur "Pop" Momand and his wife lived on Long Island in Cedarhurst, New York, in the early twentieth century. Life there was, for them, a constant struggle of trying to live "far beyond our means in our endeavor to keep up with the well-to-do class," in Momand's own words. So they rented a small apartment in Manhattan, and "Pop" used their Cedarhurst experiences as the basis for a comic strip that began to run in Joseph Pulitzer's newspaper, the *New York World,* in 1913. The comic strip depicted Aloysius and Clarice McGinis's attempts at "Keeping Up with the Joneses." Their efforts were so familiar to newly affluent Americans who were constantly comparing their wealth and status to their neighbors that the title of the strip became part of the language, and though Momand's comic creation continued to appear in American newspapers for more than twenty-eight years, the phrase has long outlasted it because we're still striving to keep up with the Joneses.

In one of the comic strips, Clarice and her husband, Aloysius, are pictured in formal evening wear. Clarice says, "Wait'll the Joneses hear we were at this swell dinner! Think of it, the Swedish ambassador is here to-night!" Aloysius sees a pompous man pass him and says, "This must be the ambassador. . . . Look at that majestic stride!" But he is shocked and embarrassed when it turns out that the majestic stride belongs to the butler.

It never fails; just when you manage to get a brand spanking new 3000 STX sports car, the guy down the street buys a *4000 STX* . . . turbocharged! And he drives it by your house at 5 a.m. every morning!

You buy a computer with a hundred-gigabyte hard drive. The week after you buy it, they come out with a *two hundred*-gig hard drive! It's enough to drive you crazy!

You can't keep up with the Joneses; they just refinanced!

In this consumer-driven society, you've got to stop comparing yourself to others; that's a trap. Paul, the great church planter of the first-century church, once said:

> We do not dare to classify or compare ourselves with [others]. When they measure themselves by themselves and compare themselves with themselves, they are not wise. (2 Cor. 10:12 NIV)

Comparing ourselves to others is a trap. First Timothy 6:9 says:

> When we long to be rich, we're a prey to temptation.
> We get trapped into all sorts of foolish and dangerous
> ambitions which eventually plunge us into ruin.
> (*Phillips*)

If you own anything—a house, a car, a wardrobe, a guitar, anything—that would just *kill you* to let go of it, you don't own it, *it* owns *you.*

So one way to throw down the idol of consumerism is to resist comparing what you have to what others have.

Rejoice

Wise King Solomon said: "It is better to be satisfied with what you have than to be always wanting something else" (Eccl. 6:9 GNB).

I happen to love the television show *Antiques Roadshow.* But it occasionally does bad things to my head; it makes me hungry for the kinds of treasures I see depicted on that show. So every once in a while I have to remind myself that there's nothing wrong with my Black and Decker coffeemaker. It is more than sufficient for my needs. I don't *need* a sterling silver Louis XIV coffeepot. I rejoice in that!

Sometimes we just have to stop and ask ourselves the tough questions like, "Will moving from a $150,000 house to a $300,000 house *double* my happiness?"

Eight years ago when my wife, the lovely Robin, and I moved our family from the first house we ever owned to the home where we now live, we went from room to room and around the yard in a little house blessing ceremony, thanking God for what we honestly believed he provided. We should probably do that every year.

One biblical writer urged: "Keep your lives free from the love of money and be content with what you have" (Heb. 13:5 NIV).

Contentment. What a novel idea! It's not easy, not when you've got hundreds of advertising messages aimed at you every day (and hundreds of thousands of dollars that have been spent on each one) to make you anything *but* content, to make you think, *I've got to have this; I've got to get that.*

But G. K. Chesterton was wise when he said there are two ways to have enough:

- Get more.
- Desire less.

So I invite you to enroll in the school of contentment. Say, "God, teach me to be satisfied with what I have rather than always wanting something else."

Refocus

The Bible says: "Set your mind on what is above, not on what is on the earth" (Col. 3:2).

If you want to overcome consumerism, you're going to have to systematically shift your focus from things below to things above, from temporal things to eternal things, from things that perish to things that are going to last forever. Dr. James Dobson once said:

> I have concluded that the accumulation of wealth even if
> I could achieve it is an insufficient reason for living.
> When I reach the end of my days, a moment or two
> from now, I must look backwards on something more
> meaningful than the pursuit of houses and lands and
> machines and stocks and bonds. Nor is fame of any last-
> ing benefit. I will consider my earthly existence to have
> been wasted unless I can recall a loving family, consistent
> investment in the lives of people, and an earnest attempt
> to serve God who made me.[6]

I challenge you to do something really risky. I challenge you to defy the myth of more, the myth that says if I get more, I'll be happier, more important, or more secure. While everybody around you may be on that track, I challenge you to be different.

If you are a Christ follower, allow me to ask you: what are you willing to do—and what are you willing to do without—in order to obey God and truly put him first in your life? Are you willing to commit at least five days to that process? Are you willing at least to begin the process of overcoming consumerism?

If you are willing, and if you have already repented of the idol of consumerism, then I urge you to walk a path of spiritual discipline over the next five days and to take on at least one spiritual exercise each of these next five days, in the following order:

Day 1: Pray for God to reveal the things you covet.

Day 2: Make a list of the things you covet.

Day 3: Prayerfully and ceremoniously destroy the list, asking God to help you let go of the desire to acquire.

Day 4: Make a new list: "Things I Can Do Without" and post it where you can add to it regularly.

Day 5: Make a new list: "Things I Can Enjoy Without Acquiring Them" (e.g., a sunrise, library books, etc.); be as creative and complete as you can be, and post the list where you can add to it regularly.

Like any spiritual discipline these simple exercises may not come easily, but they will be as effective as you are diligent in pursuing them. And as with any of the spiritual exercises yet to come in this book, it may be necessary to repeat them as many times as necessary until you begin to see the fruit of your repentance and response to God in casting down the idol of consumerism and transforming your eBay attitude.

> *God, I confess my desire to acquire. I confess that I some-*
> *times believe that having more things will make me happier,*
> *more important, or more secure. I repent of my con-*
> *sumerism. Please teach me to be grateful for what I have*
> *instead of always wanting something new or something*
> *more. Teach me to defy the myth of more and set my mind*
> *and heart on eternal things instead of material things.*
> *Teach me to keep my life free from the love of money and*
> *possessions and be content with what I have, in Jesus' name,*
> *amen.*

THREE

The Darwinian Conjecture

William Steig was an acclaimed cartoonist and author of children's books including the now-famous *Shrek*. But another of his delightful picture books is *Yellow and Pink*.

It is the story of two marionettes, two wooden string puppets, who both woke up one day to find themselves lying on an old newspaper in the hot midday sun.

In the story Yellow sits up and asks, "Do you know what we're doing here?"

Pink says, "No, I don't even remember getting here."

Pink surveys their well-formed wooden features and says, "Someone must have made us."

Yellow disagrees. "I say we're an accident." He suggests a hypothesis: A branch might have broken off a tree and fallen on a sharp rock, splitting one end of the branch into two legs. Then the wind might have sent it tumbling down a hill until it was chipped and shaped. A flash of lightning could have struck in such a way as to splinter the wood into arms and fingers. Their eyes might have been formed by woodpeckers boring in the wood. "With enough time," Yellow says, "a thousand, million, maybe two-and-a-half million years, lots of unusual things could happen. Why not us?"

The two puppets argue back and forth until finally a man comes out of a nearby house. He strolls over to the marionettes, picks them up, and checks their paint.

"Nice and dry," he murmurs approvingly, as he tucks Yellow and Pink under his arm and heads toward the house.

Peering out from under the man's arm, Yellow whispers into Pink's ear, "Who's *this* guy?"[1]

That, says Charles Colson in his excellent book *How Now Shall We Live?* is the question each of us must answer. In fact, it is the question each of us *does* answer, whether we know it or not.

But in our case, it is no quaint story; it is deadly serious. Because your answer to that question dictates the answers to the questions, Who am I? and Where do I come from? which in turn dictate the answer to the question, Where am I going?

We live in a day and age, and in the midst of a culture, that is dominated by a view called naturalism. Now don't worry if you're not sure what naturalism is. The vast majority of naturalists don't even know what it is.

Naturalism Explained

Naturalism, as simply as I can express it, is the belief that nature is all there is; everything that exists is just time, space, matter, and energy that has just naturally arisen and spontaneously developed all on its own. In the words of Carl Sagan, the most influential televangelist of naturalism since Charles Darwin himself, "The Cosmos is all that is or ever was or ever will be."[2]

In other words, there is no such thing as the *super*natural. No God. No miracles. No angels. No demons. No such thing as a human soul. It's the state of things posited by that great philosopher, John Lennon, who imagined "there's no heaven," no hell, nothing but earth and sky.

This view is nothing particularly new; three centuries before Christ, the Greek philosopher Epicurus theorized a random, purposeless naturalism that is strikingly similar to Sagan:

> The atoms in their eternal whirl, after many combinations and dissolutions, finally became united into what we call "the world." At first the earth was a lifeless lump of clay, but gradually it began to put forth grass and shrubs and flowers, just as animals and birds put forth hair and feathers. Life came next. Birds began to fly . . . and beasts prowled. . . . Some of these species were adapted to their environment and were thus enabled . . . to survive. Others were . . . the freaks of nature, the victims of a blind experiment in a planless world, and they were doomed to extinction. Man, the protagonist in this interesting play without a plot, was the last to arrive on the scene.[3]

A "blind experiment in a planless world," a "play without a plot," a marionette without a maker—that is the naturalistic view of the universe.

Of course, it's a view that never became too widespread until the late nineteenth century when a former divinity student named Charles Darwin published the landmark *The Origin of Species* and later *The Descent of Man*.

While an open-minded reading of those books will show that Darwin was not nearly as Darwinian as most twenty-first-century high school science teachers and college professors, his work nonetheless made it possible, in the famous words of British biologist Richard Dawkins, "to be an intellectually fulfilled atheist."

Still, while the impression often given by proponents of naturalism is that their conclusions are objective, proven, and fair-minded and those of religious people are obviously subjective, speculative, and biased in favor of their superstitious, unreasoning beliefs, we'll see in just a moment that it isn't necessarily so.

In contrast to naturalism, we backward, six-toed, Christ-following types actually prefer the Bible's version of "the way things really are" to that vision offered by Epicurus, Darwin, and Sagan. Like Pink in William Steig's delightful picture book, we subscribe to the view that Someone made us, that

> what may be known about God is plain to [all people], because God has made it plain to them. For since the creation of the world God's invisible qualities—his eternal power and divine nature—have been clearly seen, being understood from what has been made, so that men are without excuse. (Rom. 1:19–20 NIV)

It would be hard to find two more starkly and fundamentally contrasting views of "the way things really are." Epicurus, Darwin, and Sagan look at an orchid, an eagle in flight, the rotation of the planets, the complexity of the human eye, and they see a "blind experiment in a planless world," a "play without a plot," a random, purposeless, mindless accident; while Paul of Tarsus, Pascal,[4] and Paul Brand[5] look at those same phenomena and see "God's invisible qualities—his eternal power and divine nature."

But the line between naturalism and theism is not a line that divides scientists and saints; it's a line that runs through every one of us, practically speaking. Every time I try to get through the day "naturally" instead of prayerfully, every time I worry as if there were no God, sin as if there were no consequence, and keep my faith to myself as if there were no hell, I'm putting my money on naturalism, like a gambler putting his chips on black instead of red.

We may not worship at the feet of Charles Darwin, but the vast majority of us—even those of us who follow Christ—pay homage to the idol of naturalism every time we neglect, deny, forget, or ignore the fact that "there are more things in heaven and earth . . . than are dreamt of"[6] in our human philosophies or daily routines.

Naturalism Exposed

The proponents of naturalism, like Harvard paleontologist and Darwinian superstar Stephen J. Gould, would have us believe that science deals in facts and religion deals in faith.

Simple, right? Unless you pay attention to what they really say. For naturalism is not concerned solely with scientific fact; it is the philosophy, the bias, on which postmodern scientific pursuit relies.

Don't take it from me; take it from William Provine of Cornell University, who "declares forthrightly that Darwinism is not just about mutations and fossils; it is a comprehensive philosophy stating that all life can be explained by natural causes acting randomly—which implies that there is no need for a Creator."[7]

In fact, about Darwin himself, Charles Colson writes:

> Darwin is typically portrayed as a man forced to the theory of natural selection by the weight of the facts. But today historians recognize that he was first committed to the philosophy of naturalism and then sought a theory to justify it scientifically. Early in his career, he had already turned against the idea of creation and developed a settled conviction that, as he put it, "Everything in nature is the result of fixed laws." In other words, the deck was already stacked in favor of a naturalistic account of life before he actually uncovered any convincing facts.[8]

Not only that but Darwin's earliest apologists displayed enthusiasm for his theory not because it was good science (in fact, some of them openly disdained the science) but because they recognized it as an attractive alternative to the biblical version.

Herbert Spencer wrote: "The Special Creation belief had dropped out of my mind many years before, and I could not remain in a suspended state."[9]

And Thomas Huxley, Darwin's most famous defender, who famously called himself "Darwin's bulldog," candidly wrote:

> [Darwin] did the immense service of freeing us forever from the Dilemma—Refuse to accept the creation

hypothesis, and what have you to propose that can be
accepted by any cautious reasoner?[10]

So it is, even today. Harvard geneticist Richard Lewontin,
while candidly acknowledging the sore limitations of Darwinism,
says:

> In the struggle between science and the supernatural
> [we] take the side of science . . . because we have *a*
> *prior commitment to materialism* [that is, naturalism].[11]

In other words, despite the fact that absolutely nothing in the
history of the scientific method has been observed to come into
being without being acted upon, naturalists would still rather
believe that a natural universe naturally created itself than to
believe in a supernatural Creator.

Such reasoning is actually mentioned in the Bible. Paul the
church planter once wrote:

> For though they knew God, they did not glorify Him as
> God or show gratitude. Instead, their thinking became
> nonsense, and their senseless minds were darkened.
> Claiming to be wise, they became fools and exchanged
> the glory of the immortal God for images resembling
> mortal man, birds, four-footed animals, and reptiles.
> (Rom. 1:21–23)

You see, in typically concise and yet rich fashion, this portion of
the Bible actually depicts a sevenfold spiral into idolatry. It begins
with a refusal to glorify God and proceeds to neglecting even to
give him thanks and downward to more and more futile thinking.
When you begin from an intellectual bias that shuts out the possi-
bility of the supernatural, the transcendent, the infinite, you're lim-
iting your thinking like a detective who will consider only the facts
that support his preconceptions. Next, your heart becomes darkened and hardened, and you must more and more vehemently
claim to be wise while you become more and more foolish until
your heart, soul, and mind become thoroughly devoted to the idol
you have created for yourself.

You see? We will bow to the earth, we will bow to birds and animals and reptiles, we will bow to questionable science, even discredited or contradictory hypotheses, as long as it allows us to deny the glory of the immortal God, like the all-American farm family in the movie *The River* who sit around the dinner table and recite the prayer:

> *Thank you, earth.*
> *Thank you, sun.*
> *We are grateful*
> *for what you have done.*

Darwin's own son William said of his father: "As regards his respect for the laws of Nature, it might be called reverence if not a religious feeling."[12]

Indeed, Herbert Schlossberg, in his book *Idols for Destruction* points out:

> D. M. S. Watson, known to the public for his B.B.C. talks popularizing the Darwinian notion that human beings descended from primates, declared in an address to his fellow biologists at a Cape Town conference: "Evolution itself is accepted by zoologists not because it has been observed to occur or . . . can be proven by logically coherent evidence to be true, but because the only alternative, special creation, is clearly incredible."
>
> Similarly, the great British astronomer Sir Arthur Eddington, brooding about cosmological theories that appeared to support creation, said in 1931, "The notion of a beginning is repugnant to me." The scientific scabbards fall away to reveal ideological swords.
>
> Thomas Kuhn . . . thinks it inevitable, therefore, that a scientific group will practice its craft with a "set of received beliefs." C. S. Lewis argued that those beliefs affect the perceptions of the observer so powerfully that they control his interpretation of the empirical information he uses. That was evidently [Oswald] Spengler's meaning when he wrote that there "is no natural science without a precedent Religion."[13]

Such religious devotion reflects what the Bible calls exchanging the glory of the immortal God for the beauty and order of his Creation, a modern idolatry that shows the ancient Greeks, Romans, Canaanites, and Israelites have *nothing* on us modern, "enlightened" folk.

Because, you see, both the naturalist and the creationist believe in the uncaused Cause; the naturalist simply deifies nature, exchanging a God who sees and thinks and acts and loves for an unseeing, unthinking, unplanning, unfeeling idol, which is blind, random nature itself.

Naturalism's Effects

Some years ago a scientist named Robert Wright wrote a book called *The Moral Animal,* in which he sought to take the roulette wheel of naturalism to its logical conclusions.

According to Wright, who calls himself an evolutionary psychologist, humans are mere animals, nothing more, which is the natural result of naturalist philosophy. As with other animals, Wright says, the sole purpose of human life is to pass one's genetic code to the next generation.

This means, again according to Wright, that human males are genetically, naturally, predisposed to be sexually promiscuous because survival of the fittest is advanced by impregnating as many women as possible.

Now, of course, I have to wonder if he's married and what his wife thinks of that theory. I know without asking what *my* wife would say.

But if naturalism is "the way things really are," then Wright is correct: we are nothing more than animals, and all our thoughts and feelings, our personalities and ambitions, are simply physical and chemical reactions intended to ensure our survival.

Which means, if we bow to the idol of naturalism, we also, to be consistent, must believe of ourselves, as Professor Provine, whom I mentioned earlier, actually teaches on campuses across the United States:

> No life after death;
> no ultimate foundation for ethics;
> no ultimate meaning for life;
> no free will.[14]

That is, if you answer the question, *Where do I come from?* from a naturalist viewpoint, then you have also answered the questions, *Who am I?* and *Where am I going?* And the answers are, "An animal, a rat, a pig, a dog, no more,"[15] and, "You're going nowhere at all, no meaning in this life, and no hope for the next." Which is where all idolatry ends. As Paul wrote:

> They exchanged the truth of God for a lie, and wor-
> shiped and served something created instead of the
> Creator, who is blessed forever. Amen. . . . And because
> they did not think it worthwhile to have God in their
> knowledge, God delivered them over to a worthless
> mind to do what is morally wrong. (Rom. 1:25, 28)

God will not compel any of us to acknowledge him. He will not force us to abandon our idolatry. But he does hold out his hands to us. If we will return to him and say, "Please forgive our sins. . . . We will no longer worship the idols we have made" (Hos. 14:2–3 CEV), then he will respond: "I will heal you of your idolatry and faithlessness, and my love will know no bounds" (Hos. 14:4 NLT).

> Wherever you may be in your spiritual journey
> today, I appeal to you in the name of Jesus, turn whole-
> heartedly to the God who made you and say, "Please
> forgive [my] sins. . . . [I] will no longer worship [this
> idol I] have made." (Hos. 14:2–3 CEV)

Casting Down Your Idols

To what degree does this false god of naturalism hinder your spiritual life and growth? In order to answer that question, ponder:

- Do I habitually try to get through the day "naturally" instead of prayerfully?
- Am I prone to worry as if there were no God?
- Am I inclined to sin as if there were no consequence?
- Am I predisposed to keep my faith to myself as if there were no hell?
- Do I instinctively take credit for accomplishments and blessings instead of giving praise and thanks to God?
- When I face a problem or a challenge, is my response usually or exclusively to turn to natural resources instead of God and his supernatural resources?
- Do I have trouble truly resting in the reality of eternal life?
- Do I tend to seek my life's meaning and purpose in temporal things or eternal things?

Those are just some of the questions that may reveal the degree to which naturalism influences—even rules—your heart, mind, and life.

So how can you cast this idol out of your life? Try praying the prayer of Elisha.

You probably remember the story. The prophet Elisha had enraged the king of Aram, who sent an overwhelming force of horses, chariots, and warriors to surprise, surround, and besiege the prophet's hometown. When Elisha's servant rose the next morning, he saw the Aramean forces and panicked. "Oh, my lord," he asked Elisha, "what shall we do?"

Elisha told his servant not to be afraid, and explained,

> "Those who are with us outnumber those who are with them."
> Then Elisha prayed, "LORD, please open his eyes and let him see." So the LORD opened the servant's eyes. He looked and saw that the mountain was covered with horses and chariots of fire all around Elisha.
> (2 Kings 6:16–17)

In answer to Elisha's prayer, the servant saw beyond the natural situation and caught a glimpse of the supernatural reality, though previously he had been oblivious to it. God's prophet won a great, bloodless victory that day, and the prophet's servant learned a great lesson.

Try it. Pray at least once every day, "O Lord, open my eyes so I may see." Pray it several times a day, as you become more and more aware of your need for deliverance from the idol of naturalism. Ask him systematically, thoroughly, to deliver you from your naturalist instincts or biases and invite him to increase your awareness of his working, his intervention, and his plan in your life. Ask him to fulfill the promise, "I will heal you of your idolatry and faithlessness, and my love will know no bounds" (Hos. 14:4 NLT).

> *O Lord, open my eyes so that I may see—beginning now.*
> *Save me through and through from the idol of naturalism.*
> *Show me your hand at work in the world around me. Show*
> *me your hand at work in the people around me. Show me*
> *your hand at work in me, in Jesus' name, amen.*

FOUR

The Cowboy Ethic

Marshal Will Kane plans to hand in his badge and be on the noon train out of Hadleyville with his beautiful new wife, Amy. But his preparations are interrupted by the news that Frank Miller, an outlaw who had vowed to take revenge on the marshal who sent him to a penitentiary five years earlier, is out of prison and returning on the noon train. Frank's brother Ben and two others are waiting at the train depot for his arrival.

"Get out of this town this very minute," urges one of the townsmen. "Don't stop 'til you get to Clarksburg."

"I think I ought to stay," Kane says, but the others persuade him, and he and his wife are soon riding away in a buckboard.

But he stops. "I've got to go back," he says. "I've never run from anything in my life." And, though his wife argues, he turns them both around and heads back for town. There he plans to swear in deputies and assemble a posse to help him face the men who are coming to kill him.

But his wife, a Quaker to whom violence is unthinkable, tells him she'll be leaving on the noon train if he doesn't change his mind. The townspeople—including the judge who, just moments before, married him to Amy—refuse to be drawn into the conflict. They advise him, "You'd better go while there's still time. It's better for you, and it's better for us."

His wife can't support him, and the townspeople won't.

He's just one man. Alone. Facing four gunmen in an empty street. The train arrives. The clock ticks. The marshal writes a short will. And then, at high noon, he walks out into the dusty street of the silent town, a solitary man, implacably facing his destiny.

The Icon of Individualism

That scene, of course, is from the 1952 movie *High Noon*, starring Gary Cooper in the role of Marshal Will Kane. Gary Cooper's stoic portrayal of one man standing alone captured the imagination of the American public perhaps because it encapsulated an ideal that Americans had long before come to value: individualism.

The theme has differed only slightly throughout American history: one man against the wilderness (Daniel Boone), one man against an army (Sergeant York), one man against the Atlantic (Charles Lindbergh), one man against the sound barrier (Chuck Yeager), one man against racism (Martin Luther King Jr.), and one man against the space frontier (Neil Armstrong). Icons of individualism appear in our literature (*The Deerslayer, Moby Dick*), movies (*The Lone Ranger, Walking Tall, Cool Hand Luke*), music ("I've Gotta Be Me," "My Way"), and even in our legendary figures (Paul Bunyan and Johnny Appleseed).

Poet Robinson Jeffers captured this quintessentially American characteristic in one line:

> And you, America . . . You did not say, "en masse,"
> you said "independence."[1]

Don't misunderstand. Individual accomplishment and a healthy degree of self-sufficiency are good. But we live in a culture that has placed individualism on a high altar, and some of us are worshipping at that altar. We have minted The Cowboy Ethic, the image of one lone figure weathering the storms and riding the range, into an idol. And our worship of that idol has created a culture in which most of us live alone . . . together.

The Faces of Individualism

I've Gotta Be Me

In recent years there's been a strong emphasis in our culture on individuality, self-expression, self-esteem, and self-fulfillment. It's all about me, the individual.

"I've gotta be me." "I've got to find myself." "I've got to do what's best for me." These kinds of statements reflect one of the faces of individualism.

Think about how you would answer the question, *Who are you?* In generations past people may often have answered with descriptions like, "I'm Mike and Evelyn's daughter," or "I'm a third-generation Baptist," or even, "I'm an Okie from Muskogee." Those kinds of answers would be far less common today. It would be much more common to hear, "I'm a single woman," "I'm an Internet junkie," or "I'm a truck driver"—answers that have little or nothing to do with our communities.

Don Closson of Probe Ministries writes:

> Those afflicted [with the trait of individualism] rarely
> define themselves as part of a community, or see their
> lives in the context of a larger group. This sense of
> rugged individualism is part of the American tradition
> and has been magnified with the increased mobility of
> the last century.[2]

But you and I are communal creatures, created in the image of God, who is himself a community of persons (Father, Son, and

Holy Spirit). God put Adam in the garden of Eden, a perfect environment; but soon after giving him (seemingly) all manner of beautiful and wonderful things to enjoy, God looked at the man and said, "It is not good for the man to be alone" (Gen. 2:18).

We were made for relationships. We were created to have friends and be friends. We were designed as communal—not solely individual—creatures. Ralph C. Wood, university professor of theology and literature at Baylor University, has written:

> To be free is to conform our lives to the will and way of God. And while this freedom may begin with a sudden conversion, it cannot be sustained apart from a lifelong participation in the communal life of the people of God. To do evil, by contrast, is the really solitary and autonomous act. It is . . . to abandon the life of the self-giving love of God for our own idolatrous purposes.[3]

I Don't Need Anyone

I once asked a woman on her way into church about how I could be more helpful in involving her daughter in the youth activities of the church. She responded, "My daughter is a lot like me. She doesn't need other people in her life."

I don't remember what I said or how I responded at that moment, but I have regretted my response ever since. I regret not challenging her statement by saying something like, "My dear friend, 'You don't know the Scriptures or the power of God' (Mark 12:24). If you believe that you do not need other people and if you are teaching your daughter to believe that, then you are setting yourself up in opposition to the Word of God and ignoring his good and gracious plans for your lives.

Do you not know that *God's Word* says:

> "We were all baptized by one Spirit into one body. . . . So the eye cannot say to the hand, 'I don't need you!' nor again the head to the feet, 'I don't need you!' On the contrary, all the more. . . . God has put the body together . . . so that there would be no division in the

body, but that the members would have the same concern for each other." (1 Cor. 12:13, 21–22, 24–25)

I wish I had possessed the presence of mind and the temerity
to say to that dear woman, "If you believe that you and your
daughter don't need other people, or even that you need them
less than most folks, then you are believing a lie of the devil and
bowing to an idol of individualism."

I wish I had answered differently because a couple years after
that short conversation, that woman experienced a crisis in her
marriage and family and suffered even more greatly because
she had no network of support, no one she could confide in, no
community to comfort and care for her through her ordeal.
Those who tried were rebuffed, and it came back to me through
multiple channels that she blamed the church community she
had claimed not to need.

The fact of the matter is, we all need other people. And to
believe—or live—anything else is to abandon our wise and loving
God for an idol.

I Can Do It Myself

The path from infancy to toddlerhood is filled with gigantic,
momentous transitions: sleeping through the night, turning over
in the crib, progressing from breast-feeding or bottle-feeding to
drinking from a "sippy cup," graduating from baby food to solid
food, crawling, taking first steps, and so on. Another momentous
and healthy part of that transition is the moment when a child first
asserts, "I can do it myself!"

It's an important rite of passage, a crucial stage in human
development, to realize and assert that we are capable, apart from
parents and caretakers. But this healthy part of early child development can also be dangerous if we continue to harbor that
attitude as adults.

It's similar to an incident in Israel's history. Sometime after
they committed idolatry by making a golden calf in the Sinai

wilderness, the people complained angrily to God and Moses: "Why have you led us up from Egypt to die in the wilderness? There is no bread or water, and we detest this wretched food!" (Num. 21:5).

God responded to their ingratitude and rebellion by swarming the camp with poisonous snakes, and many of the people in the camp died. So Moses appealed to the Lord, who instructed him to erect a brass replica of the snakes on a tall pole, promising, "When anyone who is bitten looks at it, he will recover" (Num. 21:8). So Moses obeyed, and the brass serpent brought healing and deliverance to the Israelite camp that day.

But that's not the end of the story. Centuries later, when Hezekiah was Israel's king, the Bible says:

> [Hezekiah] removed the high places and shattered the
> sacred pillars and cut down the Asherah [poles]. He
> broke into pieces the bronze snake that Moses made, for
> the Israelites burned incense to it up to that time. He
> called it Nehushtan. (2 Kings 18:4)

The brass serpent was a good thing in Israel's infancy, but years later it turned dark and dangerous because they harbored it as an idol. What brought health when they were a newborn nation later led them astray.

So it is with the attitude, "I can do it myself." An independent, individualistic attitude is a rite of passage for a child but a danger for an adult. The biblical attitude is not "I can do all things," but "I can do all things *through Christ who strengthens me*" (Phil. 4:13 NKJV, italics added).

"I can do it myself" is an extremely tough lesson to unlearn, and it's certainly widespread. I am far too slow to call for help, I'm married to a strong wife who is far too slow to call for help, and I copastor with a dear friend who is far too slow to call for help! We all need to face our individualistic tendencies and more regularly let our actions reflect the truth of God's Word:

> Two are better than one because they have a good
> reward for their efforts. For if either falls, his companion

> can lift him up; but pity the one who falls without
> another to lift him up. Also, if two lie down together,
> they can keep warm; but how can one person alone keep
> warm? And if somebody overpowers one person, two
> can resist him. A cord of three strands is not easily
> broken. (Eccl. 4:9–12)

Mine! Mine! Mine!

Since before we had children, my wife, the lovely Robin, rightly dreaded three moments (among others) in each of our children's lives. (I didn't dread them as much as she did, not because I'm more serene than she is, but because I lack her keen foresight.) The moments she dreaded most were not the first few weeks of teething, or their first dates, or even the day they started to drive. No, the dreadful days she feared would come were:

- The day each of them learned to say the word *no.*
- The day they learned the concept "mine!"
- And the day they would say in anger, "I hate you."

Mercifully, wonderfully, that last day never came. But the first two did—and with a vengeance. If you're a parent, you may know how those days can change a child and, for a time at least, change the relationship between a parent and child.

It's no different with us. A typical holdover from our toddler years into our adult lives is the attitude that says, "Mine!" While the Bible does not condemn the acquisition and protection of personal property, it does make clear that the true and wholehearted worship of God is not compatible with an attitude that clings tightly to possessions and is slow to share them with others.

In fact, one of the noteworthy characteristics of the nascent Christian community immediately following Jesus' resurrection and ascension was the absence of this attitude:

> Now all the believers were together and had everything
> in common. So they sold their possessions and property
> and distributed the proceeds to all, as anyone had a
> need. (Acts 2:44–45)

We have come a long way from that attitude. But we have vastly different circumstances today, right? We have a lot more to take care of than they had back then: mortgages, cars, vacation homes, boats, investments. Which is exactly the point.

The degree to which we view our resources as "mine!" indicates the extent of our idolatry. In the early church "no one said that any of his possessions was his own" (Acts 4:32). We are just the opposite; we are loath to share our possessions and resources because we are afraid of losing them and being in need. Yet the Bible says of those first-generation Christians, "there was not a needy person among them" (Acts 4:34).

We live our lives as individuals, particularly when it comes to our possessions and resources. We may not bow to the idol of consumerism (see chapter 2), but if we take a "Mine! Mine! Mine!" attitude toward our resources, we are bowing to the idol of individualism.

The Stamp of Individualism

This American idol does not simply infect our individual lives, however. It is rampant in the church. Doug Wilson, editor of *Credenda Agenda*, writes:

> In the conservative church today, the sin that has us by the throat is individualism. And the reason it has us by the throat is that we see it as a virtue—the rugged individualism that made America great.[4]

The idol of individualism shows up in the casual approach many of us take toward the church. We shop around until we find a church we like, we attend for a while, and eventually we join. Until something happens. Perhaps the pastor failed to visit us in the hospital. Or Mrs. McKenzie in the nursery snapped at us when we were late picking up our children. Or the church grows to a point where we don't feel "at home" anymore. So we move on. We find another church. Until something happens there. And then we move on again. And through it all we are bowing to the idol of individualism instead of committing to a community and staying faithful through good times and bad.

Individualism also appears in the way we evaluate a church and its ministries. Now I know that all of us—regardless of where we are in our spiritual journeys—have real, practical needs that are only normal to try to fulfill. But it's one thing to include our needs in any evaluation of a church and its ministries; it's something else entirely never to evaluate a church any other way. I am a pastor in a wonderful church that every weekend hosts newcomers. I've answered many different questions from Christians looking for a church: Do you have a children's ministry? Do you have a youth group? How big is your women's ministry? Do you belong to a denomination? and so on. There's nothing wrong with those questions, but I've never yet had a Christian ask me, "Can this church help me fulfill my mission as a Christian?" or even "Does this church need more servants?"

Another way we bow to the idol of individualism in our churches is what Doug Wilson calls "the pietistic strain." He writes:

> Individualists on government or social issues can some-
> times be made to see that there is a deeper right than
> being right about whatever their issue is. But because
> pietists have staked out the ultimate high ground—
> communion with God, walking with Jesus, and mystic
> fellowship with the Holy Spirit—their issue trumps all
> others. . . . This usually results in setting up false stan-
> dards of holiness—you must not drink alcohol, you must
> witness every day, you must separate from churches on
> the slightest provocation.[5]

For example, I have a friend who loves God sincerely and has much to offer the church. But for five or six years, he wan-dered from church to church (and some weeks attended no church) because, he explained, "I'm an odd bird. I can't find a church that believes like me." I never found the right words to encourage him to let go of his individual "requirements" that were hindering him from committing to a Christian community. How sad, when there were any number of churches that could have benefited from his involvement.

Those are just a few of the ways individualism shows itself in our church lives.

No Man Is an Island

The idol of individualism, like all idols, not only hinders our communication with God and stunts our spiritual growth; it also deprives us of many of God's richest blessings.

A funny thing happened to me about ten years ago. I had been in public ministry, pastored three churches in the 1980s: performing weddings and funerals, visiting sick people, conducting Bible studies and small groups, coordinating outreach projects, preaching sermons, and so on and so on.

And all the time I was hiding a dirty little secret: I am an introvert. I can *function* as an extrovert, but I am a natural introvert. And through all those years of working with people, ministering to people, teaching people, visiting people, marrying and burying people, I would come home, sometimes at nine or ten o'clock, to my lovely wife, Robin.

Now she also had been ministering to people, teaching people, caring for people and caring for our kids at the same time, but she is an extrovert. So I would come in the door and she would say:

"How was your day?"

"Who did you talk to?"

"How'd the hospital visit go?"

"Do you like my hair?"

"Do you think we should paint the porch?"

"I talked to Aaron's teacher today."

"Did I tell you about Gertrude?"

"I don't think you should wear those pants again,"

and so on. And being the loving, devoted husband that I was, I would most often say, "Shhh! The game is on."

But that all changed when I started writing full-time. I would sit all day long at my desk in front of my computer in an introvert's paradise. Robin worked in an office twenty minutes away, and every evening she would come in the door at 5:30, and I would say:

"How was your day?"

"Who did you talk to?"

"How'd your presentation go?"

"Do you like my hair?"

"Do you think we should paint the porch?"

"I talked to Aaron's teacher today."

"Do you think I'm getting fat?"

and so on. That was when the realization was driven home to me that although I am an introvert by nature, I still *need* human interaction. I *need* other people. I *need* relationships. I *need* friends, fellowship, and family.

And, of course, that is also true of you. You were not made to live alone. The pastor and poet John Donne wrote:

> *No man is an island, entire of itself;*
> *every man is a piece of the continent, a part of the main.*
> *If a clod be washed away by the sea, Europe is the less,*
> *as well as if promontory were,*
> *as well as if a manor of thy friend's*
> *or of thine own were.*
> *Any man's death diminishes me,*
> *because I am involved in mankind;*
> *and therefore never send to know for whom the bell tolls;*
> *it tolls for thee.*[6]

This is true, of course, because you were created in the image of God. As Baylor University's Ralph C. Wood writes, "The triune God has revealed himself to be a community of persons who has pledged to bring us into his own life through the communal life of his people."[7] You were made to live in a community, in relationship with other people. Peter once wrote:

> God . . . has given us the privilege of being born again,
> so . . . now we are members of God's own family.
> (1 Pet. 1:3 TLB)

The church is the family of God and the antidote to the idol of individualism.

Turning from the Idol of Individualism

As with all idols the first action to take in overcoming the idol of individualism is to admit there is a problem (if you're not sure, look back at pages 47–52 and ask God to reveal to you whether your life displays any of those individualistic attitudes). Then consciously and purposely turn away from your idolatry, repent of it, and claim God's forgiveness in Jesus' name.

You might say something like:

> *Lord, I confess that I have let the idol of individualism*
> *creep into my thinking and my lifestyle. I confess that I have*
> *harbored individualistic attitudes, especially _____.*
> *I repent of those attitudes and turn from them in my heart.*
> *I come to you for cleansing and ask you to help me turn*
> *away from unhealthy and ungodly individualism. Teach*
> *me what it means to be a fully functioning, fully committed*
> *member of the family of God, the community of faith.*
> *Thank you for forgiving and restoring me, and for turning*
> *me day by day toward you and away from idols, in Jesus'*
> *name, amen.*

Having done that, consider undertaking any or all of the following exercises to counter the idol of individualism in your life:

1. Commit to change. Make a conscious commitment to pursue community with others, especially—but not exclusively—with the body of Jesus Christ, his church. Go beyond good intentions; make a firm commitment.

2. Commit to membership. If you are not a member of a local body of Christ followers, begin immediately to take steps in that direction. If you haven't been attending a church, find a church (see the appendix, "How to Find the Church That's Right for You"). If you've been attending but haven't committed yourself to membership, approach the pastor or appropriate staff member to indicate your interest in becoming a member. If you are a member of a church but have been neglecting that commitment, start this weekend to remedy that situation.

3. Commit to a small group. Community doesn't happen primarily in large groups, like your Sunday morning worship service; it's a product of small groups. That's where people learn one another's names, open up to one another, pray and cry with one another, and sometimes develop deep, lasting, intimate bonds. If you're not currently in a small group of some kind, seek one out. If your church doesn't have a small-group ministry, consider blazing the trail. If that's too scary for you, express your interest to a pastor or church leader or join a Bible study at work. But make sure it's a group that requires commitment and fosters community.

4. Commit to intentional relationships. Regardless of where you are in your knowledge of God and your relationship with Jesus Christ, you can profit enormously from seeking out and cultivating three kinds of close relationships in your life.

Though he addresses primarily men and I'd like to expand his concept to all of us, author Dr. Howard G. Hendricks suggests that each of us should seek to have three kinds of individuals in our lives: a Paul, a Barnabas, and a Timothy.[8]

A Paul is an older, more spiritually mature person who is willing to build into your life. This doesn't have to be someone who's smarter than you are, not necessarily someone who's more gifted than you are, and certainly not someone who has life all together. That person does not exist.

But you do need somebody who's been down the road you want to travel, somebody who's willing to share with you not only his strengths but also his weaknesses. Somebody who's willing to share what he or she has learned in the laboratory of life as Paul did for Timothy.

A Barnabas is a soul brother, as Barnabas was to Paul, somebody who loves you but is not impressed by you, not intimidated by you, and not fooled by you. A Barnabas is someone you can trust, someone who will love you no matter what, someone to whom you can be accountable. Hendricks writes:

> Have you got anybody in your life who's willing to keep you honest? Anybody who's willing to say to you, "Hey, man, you're neglecting your wife, and don't give me any guff! I know it, everybody else knows it; it's about time you knew it!"[9]

A Timothy is a younger person whom *you* can mentor and influence. Not that you're perfect—you're not and never will be—nor that you're some spiritual giant. But there's still someone you can influence as you yourself have been influenced. Someone to teach as you yourself have been taught. Someone to encourage as you yourself have been encouraged.

How do you find those kinds of people? First, pray that God will bring them into your life or that he will point them out to you if they're already in your life. Second, take the initiative. Look around your church, your Sunday school class, your small group, for someone who might become a Paul, a Barnabas, or a Timothy in your life. And third, just keep at it.

"Don't be surprised," Hendricks writes, "if it takes more than one or two experiences before you find that person, because there has to be a personal resonance. There's a chemistry that grows in a good mentoring relationship."[10]

5. Commit to expanding your community. If you are prone to the idol of individuality, chances are your circle of relationships has been pretty closed for some time. If you would thoroughly cast this idol out of your life, consider opening your heart and life to new relationships, perhaps even relationships that stretch you a little and introduce you to new cultures and customs. For example, you might open your home to someone who's in need of community—a new family at church, an exchange student, or recent immigrants to your country or community. You might host a party for an ESL (English as a second language) class. Or invite someone to dinner who is at a different life stage than you are. You never know when such experiences will turn into life-changing relationships.

Paul, writing about the first-century churches in Macedonia, said: "First they gave themselves to the Lord; and then, by God's will, they gave themselves to us as well" (2 Cor. 8:5 TEV).

That's how it's supposed to work: You give yourself to God, and then you become part of a community, to which you give yourself.

> *Father, thank you for revealing to me the many faces of individualism. Show me the extent of my own tendencies toward self-expression, self-exaltation, self-fulfillment, self-centeredness, self-reliance, and plain old selfishness.*
>
> *Help me to see myself in the coming days not so much as a solo performer in life, but as a member of a great chorus, a player in a symphony, a part of a Body. Help me to leave behind unhealthy and ungodly patterns of individualism. Help me not to say, "I can do it myself," but "I can do all things through Christ who gives me strength." And help me increasingly to view my money, my resources, my possessions, and my church through the prism of the community to which I belong, in Jesus' name, amen.*

FIVE

The Rock Star Syndrome

I once asked a number of my friends if they'd ever met a celebrity. The answers were intriguing.

My friend Leslye Simak once met Hillary Clinton, who seemed to act a little wary as Leslye approached her. But, it may be inferred, once Mrs. Clinton felt safe that Leslye wasn't part of a vast right-wing conspiracy, she was quite pleasant to Leslye.

My friend Dawn Owens met President Clinton, and she says she has pictures to prove it.

Another friend, Henry Saas, acted in a play with John Goodman of *Roseanne* fame, which made me wonder: *If John had just invited Henry to play the part of Roseanne's sister's boyfriend, maybe Henry could be George Clooney by now!*

My friend Bob Holzworth ate lunch with Jodie Foster and Diane Weist; he says they ignored him, but he was there!

Amber Bennett met Sean Connery and Princess Anne on the same day in the town of Sleat on the Isle of Skye—all of which sounds so incredibly cool!

Mark Fitzgerald once met the late Dave Thomas of Wendy's fame, Daryl and Gretchen Zimmer met NBA star David Robinson, Mike Johnson met Neil Armstrong, and Phil Schreiber met Steven Covey of the *Seven Habits of Highly Successful People.* And I once stood a mere four feet from Joe Piscopo at the Newark airport baggage claim, frantically wracking my brain to think of something more intelligent to say than, "Dude! You're Joe Piscopo!" I never did.

All those celebrity moments among my little circle of friends: a princess, a president, a senator, an astronaut, actors, authors, and athletes. I was astonished. Amazed. Flabbergasted, even.

Less amazing is the fact that each of those people remembers that celebrity encounter. Some remember them like they happened just yesterday. Some may remember them until the day they die. Which illustrates another typically American idol, one I call the Rock Star Syndrome: celebrity worship.

A New Kind of Eminence

Pastor and author Tony Evans writes, in the introduction to his book *Who Is This King of Glory?*

> We live in a day of celebrity worship. . . . Celebrities grab
> our attention. People want to get close to them, to get
> an autograph or even a glimpse of the famous person.[1]

And even before the dawn of *The Anna Nicole Show,* Daniel Boorstin, the social historian, wrote:

> Our age has produced a new kind of eminence. This is
> as characteristic of our culture and our century as was
> the divinity of Greek gods in the sixth century BC. . . .
> This new kind of eminence is "celebrity." The hero is
> made by folklore, sacred texts and history books but the
> celebrity is the creature of gossip . . . of magazines,
> newspapers and the ephemeral images of movie and tele-
> vision screen. . . . Anyone can become a celebrity if only
> he can get into the news and stay there.[2]

The number of magazines, Web sites, books, and television shows devoted to celebrities has exploded since the 1974 launch of *People Magazine* and the 1981 debut of *Entertainment Tonight*. And our culture's fascination with celebrities shows no sign of letting up anytime soon.

Not long ago Brooklyn high school students were asked in a questionnaire, "What would you like to be?" Two-thirds answered: "a celebrity." Not "astronaut." Not "president." Not even "rock star." Just "a celebrity."

Our worship of celebrities has recently reached new highs (or lows, depending on how you look at it): a bidder on eBay recently paid $455 for three tablespoons of water reportedly touched by Elvis Presley at a 1977 concert. Maria Puente, writing in *USA Today,* reports:

> In recent years, people have tried or succeeded in auctioning chewing gum said to have been discarded by Britney Spears; a cough drop supposedly spit out by Arnold Schwarzenegger; what are said to be the baby teeth of Jack Nicholson; and the dirty socks of Bryan Adams.[3]

It happens no less among those of us who call ourselves Christ followers. We have a tendency to idolize famous authors, famous preachers, famous singers, not primarily because of what they say or how God is using them but because they're famous. And sometimes we rush from church to church or conference to conference following not God but the "anointing" we believe that person has.

Marva Dawn, in her book *Reaching Out without Dumbing Down,* writes:

> [We are prone to] the idolatrous adulation of "famous" Christians. . . . Instead of recognizing the value of their own daily experience of following Jesus, some believers falsely elevate big-name stars or let others do the ministry. As a result, performers of contemporary Christian music and hyped-up speakers and writers are elevated to celebrity status. . . .

The danger of such "fame" became apparent to me
several years ago when a teenager who had heard me
speak at a large youth convention saw me in a store in
Portland and begged for my autograph. I asked her why
my signature was more valuable than hers. We are all
equally significant members of the Body of Christ, are
we not? We all have crucial parts to play in the church's
ministry to the world. The church should be the last
place where anyone is thought to be more important
than anyone else.[4]

Many celebrities, Christian or otherwise, make great music,
write riveting books, play great roles on the movie screen, or excel
in one sport or another, entertaining, informing, or impressing us
with some ability or characteristic. But so do many noncelebrities,
who should be no less interesting to us.

And how do you explain our fascination with other cele-
brities—like Rupert Boneham (of *Survivor*), Paris Hilton, Monica
Lewinsky, Kato Kaetelin, Joey Buttafuoco, Pia Zadora, Tiny
Tim—oh, now I'm showing my age!

Why do we find celebrities so interesting, so captivating? Why
is our culture so driven by celebrity? What's it all about? Does it
even matter? And what does it hurt?

That's a lot of questions, so let's slow down a bit and let me
suggest to you three possible reasons that we as a culture and as
individuals are so quick to engage in celebrity worship.

A Longing for Community

Say what? You may well ask.

What could celebrity worship have to do with a longing for
community? As Ricky Ricardo might say, "I can esplain."

According to the Bible, when God created human beings,
he created us as communal creatures. As we discussed in chapter 4,
God makes us individuals, but he doesn't intend for us to be
individual*ists*.

Way back in the first few pages of the Bible, "The Lord God said, 'It is not good for the man to be alone'" (Gen. 2:18).

But these modern times, the way we live our lives these days, are not terribly conducive to real community: In most twenty-first-century communities, there's no town square, no communal watering hole, so to speak, no "Third Place," as sociologists are calling it now (that is, we all have homes and workplaces, but for many of us there's no Third Place, no place where we routinely go just to chew the fat, let our hair down, and experience the joys of community).

Because most of us don't have such a place, and as our lives revolve more and more around work, more and more focused on a computer screen until our only interaction with other human beings some days is over the telephone, e-mail, instant messenger, or chat room, it eventually gets to the point where we feel like our most enduring, most faithful friendships are with people named Ross, Joey, Chandler, Rachel, Phoebe, and Monica!

But as our relationships become more disjointed and inter-action with friends becomes less frequent, we come to thrive on news of this star or that celebrity *as if we knew them!* Down deep we'd much rather have *real* people to talk about, catch up on, and incorporate into our lives, but in their absence we'll often settle for the false community of celebrity worship without even realizing what we're doing.

Still, in the end it's empty, unsatisfying, "utterly meaning-less," as King Solomon said. It's a poor substitute for true com-munity, the kind of community each of us was made for, the kind we hunger for until we experience it, the kind the Bible, God's Word, talks about when it says, about all who follow Christ:

> You are no longer foreigners and aliens, but fellow citi-zens with God's people and members of God's house-hold, built on the foundation of the apostles and prophets, with Christ Jesus himself as the chief corner-stone. In him the whole building is joined together and rises to become a holy temple in the Lord. And in him

> you too are being built together to become a dwelling
> in which God lives by his Spirit. (Eph. 2:19–22 NIV)

The community we all long for is not found in celebrity worship but in uniting with others in the worship of God and loving and being loved in a family of faith.

So one possible reason we are so quick to engage in celebrity worship is a longing for community. Another reason may be a longing for significance.

A Longing for Significance

Maria Puente, writing in *USA Today*, asks:

> Why . . . would Chas Welch, 31, of Atlanta, frame a
> napkin from Prince's 1996 wedding, which is printed
> with the mysterious symbol the rock star was using as
> his name? "It's a connection to the person that no one
> else can have," Welch says. "That's what motivates
> collectors—they want that feeling that they're the most
> important person in the world."[5]

Think about how you would act if you walked into your local Baskin-Robbins tonight and got in line behind Tiger Woods. What would you do, really?

Whatever else you might do, you'd probably say to the first two dozen friends or acquaintances you ran into, "Guess who *I* just saw in Baskin-Robbins?"

And after you told them, they would say, "You met Tiger Woods? Wow!"

"Yep," you might say next, "he and I go way back."

What's that about? Why are we so anxious to tell others when we see or meet someone famous? It doesn't make *us* famous. It doesn't make us important or significant. It's not like Tiger Woods is going to go home and say to *his* friends, "Guess who *I* just saw in Baskin-Robbins?"

But, of course, when we tell our friends and family about our brush with fame, what happens?

They say, "Really?"

"What was it like?"

"What did you do?"

"Hey, Peggy, tell Phyllis who you saw in Baskin-Robbins."

And suddenly people are listening to us and paying attention to us and making over us. And that momentarily satisfies our longing for significance.

We all want to be important to somebody. We all want to be valuable in someone's eyes. We all want to be significant, some way, some day.

But after a day or two of telling the story, what happens?

"Did I mention who I saw in Baskin-Robbins?"

"Yeah, yeah, Tiger Woods, you told me."

It's old news. But it was fun while it lasted, right? Well, guess what?

You don't have to meet a celebrity to be significant.

You already are.

The Bible says that: "God sent his One and Only Son into the world so that [you] might live through him" (1 John 4:9).

That means, in God's eyes, *you* are worth the lifeblood of his only Son. That's the measure of your significance! And if you are a Christ follower, the Bible says that you are God's poem, his masterpiece (see Eph. 2:10). It says that you are part of "a chosen race, a royal priesthood, a holy nation, a people for His possession" (1 Pet. 2:9).

That is true significance, the kind that never fades, never diminishes, never changes. So it may be that we are so quick to engage in celebrity worship because we have a longing for community and a longing for significance. A third and final reason may be that we have a deep, abiding longing for glory.

A Longing for Glory

Sometimes I think our worship of celebrities is an intimation, a hint of our longing for glory, our yearning for immortality.

The Bible says: "God has . . . planted eternity in the human heart" (Eccl. 3:11 NLT).

And fame offers a counterfeit immortality, as expressed in the theme song of the eighties TV show *Fame*: "Fame! I'm gonna live forever!" And even if *we* aren't celebrities, we want a connection with someone who's going to "live forever."

You know, if I can't be the sun, I'll settle for the moon. If I can't have glory of my own, I'll settle for reflected glory.

But going down in history is *nothing* like going on for eternity. And that's what the Bible says is available to us, to those of us who trust Christ. The Bible says that "Christ in you"—*not* some celebrity, some famous person, but Christ in you—is your "hope of glory" (Col. 1:27).

> [For though] what we will be has not yet been made
> known . . . we know that when he appears, we shall be
> like him, for we shall see him as he is. (1 John 3:2 NIV)

This rock star syndrome, our fascination with celebrities, our tendency to worship the famous, this typically American idol, cannot deliver the goods.

Like the idols of old, celebrity worship "is trusting something that can give [us] no help at all. Yet [we] cannot bring [ourselves] to ask, 'Is this thing, this idol . . . a lie?'" (Isa. 44:20 NLT).

It *is* a lie.

It is an idol.

And it is a poor substitute, as all idols are, for the reality, the substance, the truth that is available to us in Jesus Christ.

The Measure of the Malady

Recent studies by a team of researchers from American and British universities identified a psychiatric condition they have dubbed "celebrity worship syndrome." They estimate, based on the studies, that roughly a third of the American population exhibits an unhealthy interest in celebrities.

They even devised a "celebrity worship scale" of three levels
from mild to serious:

- *Entertainment social:* This is casual stargazing. The
  level of celebrity worship here is really quite mild:
  "My friends and I like to discuss how Ben could
  have moved from Gwyneth to J. Lo."

- *Intense personal:* The person seems to feel a connection with the star: "I consider Halle Berry to
  be my soul mate."

- *Borderline pathological:* Here, admiration has gone
  stalker-esque: "When he reads my love letters,
  Brad Pitt will leave Jennifer Aniston and live
  happily ever after with me."[6]

- Your interest in celebrities may not even make that list,
  but that doesn't necessarily mean you're clean. You may
  ask yourself: "Do I buy or read everything I can about a
  certain celebrity? Do I give more weight to political or
  spiritual opinions of celebrities? Do I feel an emotional
  attachment to a celebrity or star? Have I ever gotten
  happy or sad because of an event in a celebrity's life or
  career? Do I ever betray a belief that meeting or knowing
  someone famous would make my life more meaningful?
  Do I know more about any celebrity's life than I do
  about the life of Jesus? Do I spend more time reading
  celebrity or entertainment magazines than my Bible or
  devotional material? Do I tend to talk more (or more
  excitedly) about the latest movies or music than my latest
  encounters with God, his Word, and his people?"

- These questions are not necessarily indications that you're
  clinically idolatrous! And they certainly should not be
  viewed as some legalistic standard ("you should read your
  Bible more than you read *Entertainment Weekly*"). But
  they may allow the Holy Spirit of God to shine a light into

a corner of your heart and show you an area where you have erected an idol.

A Celebrity Remedy

So how can you counter even minor tendencies toward celebrity worship? Here's one suggestion: celebrate Communion, the ceremony in which we remember Jesus' dying love for sinners like you and me. Do it as soon as possible, and as frequently as possible, reminding yourself as you do that you are actually signifying the reality that celebrity worship merely counterfeits. As you celebrate at the Lord's table, remind yourself that with your grateful acceptance of the bread and the cup you are saying:

- I belong.

Because Jesus died for you,

> You . . . are among those who are called to belong to
> Jesus Christ (Rom. 1:6 NIV),

and you are among "those who belong to the family of believers" (Gal. 6:10 NIV). When you eat the bread and drink from the cup, it should tell you also:

- I matter.

> For you know that it was not with perishable things
> such as silver or gold that you were redeemed from the
> empty way of life handed down to you from your fore-
> fathers, but with the precious blood of Christ
> (1 Pet. 1:18–19 NIV).

That's how much you matter to God. That's the measure of your significance. That's the extent of your worth. And, finally, when you eat the bread and drink from the cup, it should tell you:

- I will be glorified.

> For as often as you eat this bread and drink the cup,
> you proclaim the Lord's death until he comes
> (1 Cor. 11:26),

and

> When [Jesus] the Messiah, who is your life, is revealed,
> then you also will be revealed with Him in glory.
> (Col. 3:4)

As you intentionally and successfully remind yourself through the gift of the sacrament that you belong, you matter, and you will appear with Christ in glory, you will be tearing down the idol of celebrity worship in your mind, heart, and life. No idol can invade a heart that is already full.

> *Awesome God, I confess my interest in celebrities and stars, and repent of too often fixing my eyes on them instead of on Jesus, the author and perfecter of my faith (see Heb. 12:2). Please empty my heart of all its fascination with celebrities. Show me that in you, I belong. Teach me that in you I matter. And impress upon me that in you I will be glorified. Fill my heart so much with your glory and grace that all the things of this earth will grow dim, in Jesus' name, amen.*

SIX

The Microwave
Mentality

It was the early nineties, and my wife, the lovely Robin, and I were foster parents to six teenage boys in a group home setting. Our boys, between the ages of twelve and seventeen, had come to us from the juvenile court system.

You could say that each was there for a different reason. One had been involved in a few minor scrapes with the law but was sent to us after intentionally throwing a skateboard under a city bus, causing an accident. (He did it, he said, just to "see what would happen.") Another had been repeatedly truant. Another couldn't stop experimenting with drugs. Another had been convicted of a sexual offense.

But as we got to know and love "our boys," we eventually learned that, in another sense, every one of them was there for the same reason: the inability to postpone gratification. Each of them displayed a strikingly predictable weakness: given the choice between obtaining or enjoying something now or later, they would always choose "now." Even if the reward would be substantially bigger "later." I tested it many times, and the result was always the same.

"Brian," I would say, "how would you like a Hershey bar right now?"

"Sure," he would answer.

"What if I gave you a choice? What if I said you could have one Hershey bar now or two Hershey bars after dinner? Which would you choose?"

"I want it now," he would say.

I tried upping the ante, so to speak.

"Shane," I would say, "you've earned an extra hour of television privileges today."

"All right!" he would say.

"But if you wait till next week, I'll give you an extra hour every day."

I could see the wheels turning. I could see he was tempted. But I could see it was just too much to ask.

"No," he would say. "That's OK. I want to watch *Perfect Strangers* tonight."

"But it'll be on next week," I would say.

He would smile sheepishly. "That's OK."

Now or Later

In 1962 the Phoenix Candy Company released a new concept in candy called "Now and Later." Each package consisted of several individually wrapped taffy squares, and the candy was available in a dozen flavors (apple, banana, cherry, grape, orange, pineapple, etc.). The candy was called "Now and Later" to suggest to customers that they could eat some of the taffy squares immediately and save the rest for later.

But that's not how we tend to operate—especially not as children, right? Most of us who enjoyed Now and Laters ate them pretty quickly. One woman even recalls, "I remember at eight years old, I used to get my allowance, and on the way to school

I would go to our general store (Ivan's in Duquesne, Pennsylvania) and buy a pack of pineapple Now and Laters. I would unwrap each of them and put them all in my mouth at one time and chew for days. It's the best and only way to eat them!"[1]

That's pretty much how I acted as an eight-year-old. That's how "our boys" would have eaten Now and Laters. That's how most people would do it.

In the 1960s behavioral scientists at Stanford University in California conducted a series of studies. They would sit a preschooler at a table and place a single marshmallow in front of the child. They would explain to the child that he or she could eat the marshmallow immediately or wait fifteen minutes and get two marshmallows! Predictably, most of the children decided that a marshmallow in the hand is worth two in the future.

That wasn't the end of the study, however. The researchers tracked those children for the next decade and found that the children who had waited for the second marshmallow were happier and more successful as teenagers. They were less prone to give in to peer pressure, less likely to panic under stress. They tended to be more self-reliant, confident, and trustworthy than those children who had trouble postponing gratification.

Our Microwave Mentality

What was once true mainly of children has become the rule throughout our society. We eat fast food, ride rapid transit, use instant coffee, bank at drive-through windows, service our cars at Jiffy Lube, make copies at Quick Print, pick up a gallon of milk at the Quick Stop Shop, ship packages overnight, dry clean our clothes at the One-Hour Cleaners, pay extra for high-speed Internet, pay for gas purchases with a quick wave of our SpeedPass, and speed through toll plazas with E-ZPass.

We do not simply *prefer* instant gratification; we *demand* it. How else can we explain our indignation when our lunch-hour pizza isn't served within *five minutes* of our arrival at the restaurant table? How else can we explain our impatience after *four minutes* of waiting in line at the bank, our inability to endure *three minutes* of television commercials without reaching for the remote control, or our rage when a Web site takes as much as ten seconds to upload?

Like the children in the marshmallow experiment, of course, some of us are less prone to demand instant gratification than others among us. But some of us have let this childish desire grow into an adult expectation. Some of us have become so accustomed to getting what we want when we want it that we find it difficult to postpone gratification, even in small things and unimportant areas of life. Some of us have nursed and coddled our desire for quick results until it has grown into what *Entrepreneur Magazine* has called "the idol of our society: instant gratification."[2]

So how can you determine whether the drive for instant gratification is an idol—or in danger of becoming an idol—in your life? Try honestly to answer these questions:

- Do I buy things on credit simply because I want them now?
- Do I get discouraged and give up if I don't see quick results in dieting, studying, saving, etc.?
- Am I prone to take shortcuts in my job, relationships, and spiritual life?
- Do I tend to stop praying for something when God doesn't answer quickly?
- Do I have trouble waiting for mealtimes to eat?
- When I'm contemplating a large purchase, do I often make a decision too quickly because I don't want to wait any longer?
- Do I get angry when I have to wait in line?
- Do I tend to value quick results more than quality?
- When is the last time I knowingly postponed gratification?
- Do I expect my times of prayer and worship to bring quick results, or do I persevere even when I seem to be deriving no immediate benefit?

- Do I give regularly to God and the church, or do my stewardship and service change according to what I'm getting out of it?

Your answers to these questions may not fully reveal whether you have exalted "instant gratification" to the level of an idol. But if you take them seriously, these questions may lead to others, and the process of self-examination may be the means God uses to reveal and rescue you from taking a path similar to the one that led to King Saul's destruction.

An Easy Road to the Top

King Saul was a golden boy. Even as a young man, "he stood a head taller than anyone else" (1 Sam. 10:23). Samuel the prophet said, "There is no one like him among the entire population" (1 Sam. 10:24). Good things, incredible things, just seemed to come to him. One day he was out looking for lost donkeys, and the next day he was prophesying like Samuel and anointed as king over all Israel (1 Sam. 10).

Saul began well. He apparently started out with an attitude of humility. When the famous prophet Samuel met Saul in the land of Zuph, Samuel said, "When I send you off in the morning, I'll tell you everything that's in your heart. . . . And who does all Israel desire but you and all your father's family?" (1 Sam. 9:19–20). But Saul responded, "Am I not a Benjaminite from the smallest of Israel's tribes and isn't my clan the least important of all the clans of the Benjaminite tribe? So why have you said something like this to me?" (1 Sam. 9:21). In other words, "Why would you be so kind and generous to me, who comes from such humble roots?"

Saul also started out in vulnerability. Having anointed Saul to be king, Samuel called all the tribes of Israel to send representatives to a solemn gathering at Mizpah. There,

Samuel had all the tribes of Israel come forward, and the tribe of Benjamin was selected. Then he had the tribe of Benjamin come forward by its clans, and the Matrite clan was selected. Finally, Saul son of Kish was selected. But when they searched for him, they could not find him. They again inquired of the LORD, "Has the man come here yet?"

The LORD replied, "There he is, hidden among the supplies."

They ran and got him from there. (1 Sam. 10:20–23)

Saul probably heard Samuel scold the Israelites at Mizpah. "Today you have rejected your God, who saves you from all your troubles and afflictions. You said to Him, 'You must set a king over us'" (1 Sam. 10:19). Saul likely recognized that as an inauspicious beginning for the monarchy. He might well have been afflicted with cold feet when he realized that he, a mere man, was being installed as king over a nation that had just fired God Almighty from the job! (Talk about a tough act to follow!) And apparently, aware of his vulnerable position, he hid himself in the supplies the various caravans had brought to the ceremony, hoping they would start the party without him.

Saul not only started out in humility and vulnerability. He also began his reign with an admirable share of mercy. After Samuel installed Saul as the new king,

Samuel sent all the people away, each to his own home.

Saul also went to his home in Gibeah. . . . But some wicked men said, "How can this guy save us?" They despised him and did not bring him a gift, but Saul said nothing. . . .

Afterwards, the people said to Samuel, "Who said that Saul should not reign over us? Give us those men so we can kill them!"

But Saul ordered, "No one will be executed this day, for today the LORD has provided deliverance in Israel." (1 Sam. 10:25–27; 11:12–13)

The path Saul took in becoming king of Israel was a fairly smooth one. But it was soon to become a bad trip. Maybe he became too accustomed to the easy road. Maybe the way good things just seemed to fall into his lap allowed him to become king without developing the kind of faith and commitment which later events would require. Maybe he became susceptible to a form of idolatry that our culture and age makes us prone to.

Instant Gratification in Gilgal

In what must have been a whirlwind of events, Saul became king of Israel and commander of Israel's armies. But he soon found himself with a "situation" on his hands. His son, Jonathan, had attacked the Philistine garrison in Geba, an act that Saul expected would start an all-out war.

So he sent out the call through the tribes of Israel to muster his armies:

> Then the troops were summoned to join Saul at Gilgal.
> The Philistines also gathered to fight against Israel: 3,000 chariots, 6,000 horsemen, and troops as numerous as the sand on the seashore. They went up and camped at Michmash, east of Beth-aven.
> The men of Israel saw that they were in trouble because the troops were in a difficult situation. They hid in caves, thickets, among rocks, and in holes and cisterns. Some Hebrews even crossed the Jordan to the land of Gad and Gilead.
> Saul, however, was still at Gilgal, and all his troops were gripped with fear. (1 Sam. 13:4–7)

It was clearly a desperate situation. Saul and his armies were outnumbered. His troops were scared. Many deserted. But Saul had an ace in the hole, so to speak. He had a secret weapon. Samuel, the prophet who had anointed him, had earlier promised

to meet Saul there in Gilgal, to sacrifice offerings to God and tell
Saul "what to do" (1 Sam. 10:8).

That situation is the setting for three things that are typically
part of the path we will travel each time we bow down to the idol
of instant gratification.

Stressful Circumstances

Stressful circumstances are not the only soil in which this particular form of idolatry grows. The man or woman who is prone
to this form of idolatry can certainly display "the microwave mentality," the desire for instant gratification, at any time. But stressful circumstances will tend noticeably to accentuate and accelerate
that tendency.

That's clearly what happened at Gilgal. Remember the setting. Philistines coming. Lots of chariots and horsemen. Bajillions
of soldiers. Saul's troops start to feel queasy. "I hear my mama
calling," some say. "I just thought of someplace I have to be,"
explain others. And the few that are left behind with Saul have a
bad case of butterflies in the stomach.

But Samuel is coming, right? Samuel the prophet. The man of
God. He's even promised to tell Saul "what to do." So Saul waits.

And waits.

And waits.

Samuel said seven days. It's been seven days. But Samuel still
hasn't shown up. The Bible account says:

> [Saul] waited seven days for the appointed time that
> Samuel had set, but Samuel didn't come to Gilgal, and
> the troops were deserting him. So Saul said, "Bring me
> the burnt offering and the fellowship offerings." Then
> he offered the burnt offering. (1 Sam. 13:8–9)

Who can blame him, right? Sure, Samuel (the man of God)
had said to wait. Sure, Samuel had said *he* (not Saul) would offer
the burnt offering and the fellowship offerings. Sure, the day was

not over yet. But Saul's blood pressure was rising, and his troops were deserting him.

Such stressful circumstances all too often lead us into temptation. Such situations often lead us into sin by prompting us to forget who is in control. We forget that God is still God, and his Word is still sure.

On those rare occasions when our sea of life is calm, we can more easily postpone gratification and make wise decisions. When the sun is shining and "all's right with the world," we can more readily remember that "God is in his heaven." When our path is smooth, we're not so apt to slide into the soft idolatry of instant gratification. No, it's under the pressure of stressful circumstances that we are likely to place our immediate wants and needs on a higher shelf than what God has commanded or promised.

Selfish Impatience

God was not twiddling his thumbs while Saul chewed his fingernails at Gilgal. Samuel, coming from Ziph, would have started out on his journey to Gilgal a few days in advance. But Saul, though God had handpicked him, lifted him from obscurity, and transformed him into royalty, could not imagine that God could triumph without Saul's help. Israel's king saw the men deserting left and right and could not imagine Israel's God overcoming their circumstances . . . unless something was done and done fast.

> So Saul said, "Bring me the burnt offering and the
> fellowship offerings." Then he offered the burnt
> offering.
>   Just as he finished offering the burnt offering,
> Samuel arrived. So Saul went out to greet him,
> and Samuel asked, "What have you done?"
> (1 Sam. 13:9–11)

It's interesting that the first words appear to have been Samuel's: "What have you done?" Perhaps the king met the prophet with a defensive, "What took you so long?" Maybe Saul greeted Samuel with a relieved, "I'm so glad you made it safely!" Or maybe the first words they exchanged, though unrecorded, were a reflexive "I can explain" from Saul. But no matter who spoke first, the first words the account reports are Samuel's: "What have you done?"

> Saul answered, "When I saw that the troops were deserting me and you didn't come within the appointed days and the Philistines were gathering at Michmash, I thought: The Philistines will now descend on me at Gilgal, and I haven't sought the LORD's favor. So I forced myself to offer the burnt offering."
> (1 Sam. 13:11–12)

There are times in our lives when stressful circumstances press down on us and we become impatient for God to act, for his answer to come, for his promise to show up. And if he delays, we lose faith. Like Saul we see only the circumstances ("the troops") and the delay ("you didn't come"), and in so doing we forget ourselves; or, more accurately, we forget God. We forget his promise never to leave us or forsake us (see Heb. 13:5). We forget his promise to be with us through the deepest waters and the fiercest trials (see Isa. 43:2). We forget his promise to supply all our needs (see Phil. 4:19).

At the root of our impatient drive for instant gratification is a lack of faith in God. Our selfish impatience springs from a fear that God will not keep his promises to us, that he will not provide for us, that he will not show up when we need him. So, like Saul, we "force" ourselves to act and take matters into our own hands. And it is always a form of rebellion and idolatry to take matters out of God's hands and into our own.

Sinful Defiance

Once Samuel arrived in Saul's camp, all the hapless king could do was to try to put the best face possible on his actions. He tried to tell Samuel that he was still seeking the Lord and depending on him; he just had to force himself to improvise and offer the burnt offering without Samuel. But Samuel (he was a prophet, after all) saw right through it:

> Samuel said to Saul, "You have been foolish. You have not kept the command which the LORD your God gave you. It was at this time that the LORD would have permanently established your reign over Israel, but now your reign will not endure. The LORD has found a man loyal to Him, and the LORD has appointed him as ruler over His people, because you have not done what the LORD commanded." (1 Sam. 13:13–14)

Wow, that seems really harsh, doesn't it? Wasn't Saul doing the best he knew how? Wasn't he still sacrificing to God? Wasn't he just finding a different way to sacrifice to God and seek his favor? Wasn't it a bit extreme for God to retract his plans to make Saul's family into a dynasty in Israel?

The answer to all the above is no. Samuel's rebuke makes clear that Saul's hastiness was no honest miscalculation; it was disobedience. It was rebellion. It was idolatry.

So it is with us. When we let selfish impatience—even in the midst of stressful circumstances—lure us into forgetting God's commands or his promises and fulfilling our desire for instant gratification, we are no longer sacrificing to God or serving him. We are idolaters.

Now, don't misunderstand. It's not necessarily a sin to satisfy a simple craving or do something now instead of later. It may even be virtuous (if we're avoiding procrastination, for instance). But when our demand for instant gratification prompts us to take matters out of God's hands and into our own, to run ahead of God instead of following faithfully, to try to hurry God instead of waiting on him, then we have stopped serving God and begun sacrificing to an idol—the idol of instant gratification.

Can I wait for the Lord, even when he delays? Can I believe that God will provide for me, even when the bills pile up? Can I hope that he will send me a godly mate, even if I haven't had a date in months? Can I stay faithful even when my ministry efforts seem to wither on the vine? Can I look forward to God's vindication, even when my reputation is being trashed? Can I trust in his good plans for me, even when I've had a disastrous reversal of fortune? Will I grasp or trust? Will I hurry or wait? Will I charge or save? Will I fast or binge? Will I doubt or hope?

Idolatry's Offspring

Saul's idolatry produced disastrous results, as idolatry routinely does. But it's the experience of another Bible character, the patriarch Abraham, that most vividly depicts for us the fruit of this pursuit of instant gratification.

Abraham (or Abram, at first) was a friend of God. God had told him, "Do not be afraid, Abram. I am your shield, your very great reward" (Gen. 15:1 NIV).

God promised him that, though he and his wife Sarai were childless, and old, he would have many descendants "from your own body" (Gen. 15:4). And "Abram believed the LORD" (Gen. 15:6).

But time passed. Nothing happened. God seemed silent. Abram and Sarai must have faced temptation many times, but one day changed everything:

> Abram's wife Sarai had not borne him children. She
> owned an Egyptian slave named Hagar. Sarai said to
> Abram, "Since the LORD has prevented me from bearing
> children, go to my slave; perhaps I can have children by
> her." And Abram agreed to do what Sarai said. So
> Abram's wife Sarai took Hagar, her Egyptian slave, and
> gave her to her husband Abram as a wife for him. . . .
> He slept with Hagar, and she became pregnant.
> (Gen. 16:1–4a)

Problem solved, right? Of course not. Abram and Sarai's attempt to take matters out of God's hands and into their own bore nothing but bitter results:

> When [Hagar] realized that she was pregnant, she
> looked down on her mistress. Then Sarai said to Abram,
> "You are responsible for my suffering! I put my slave
> in your arms, and ever since she knew that she was
> pregnant, she has looked down on me. May the LORD
> judge between me and you."
>   Abram replied to Sarai, "Here, your slave is in your
> hands; do whatever you want with her." Then Sarai
> mistreated her so much that she ran away from her.
> (Gen. 16:4b–6)

The pursuit of instant gratification produced nothing but bitter fruit for Abram, Sarai, Hagar, and even Hagar's son, who would be named Ishmael. And so it will be for us. Our "microwave mentality" will produce nothing but bitter fruit in our lives:

- It short-circuits God's timing and further delays his good plans for us. Far from helping God along, Abram and Sarai probably delayed the fulfillment of his promise to them by their faithless "Hagar strategy" because it is "through faith and patience [that we] inherit what has been promised" (Heb. 6:12 NIV).
- It impedes our spiritual growth and warps our character, instead of developing "by experience [our] power to discriminate between what is good and what is evil" (Heb. 5:14 Phillips).
- It is sometimes the cause of our struggles with obesity; 61 percent of Americans are overweight, and as our stressful circumstances increase, so do our waistlines.
- It creates division and shatters relationships, as Abram and Sarai experienced. As psychologist Howard J. Rankin says, "The requirements for a loving relationship run completely counter to the mentality of an instant, disposable and user-friendly society. We are bombarded with messages about ease and convenience but come home to relationships that simply do not work."[3]
- It can plunge us into debt. "Buy now, pay later" is a great strategy—for retailers and credit card companies. But it

traps millions in a cycle of debt that for some ends only in bankruptcy.

- It can even prevent God from fulfilling all his good plans for our lives, as Saul found out when he offered hasty sacrifices and so forfeited an enduring dynasty.
- And, like all idolatry, the "microwave mentality" makes us less like the one true God and more like the false god we serve. As long as we serve the idol of "instant gratification," our lives will tend to display less patience, less self-discipline, and less faith.

Overcoming the Microwave Mentality

It is no coincidence that Jesus' temptations in the wilderness were all temptations to instant gratification. The devil tried to entice him with the promise of bread now (instead of later), glory now (instead of later), and power now (instead of later).[4] Certainly Jesus knew that he would eat again, and he had to know that he would receive power and glory again after completing his mission. But the temptation to hurry things along was no less severe for all that. And his victory over the lure of instant gratification also provides guidance for us in overcoming the "microwave mentality."

Like all forms of idolatry, our first task is to recognize and repent, consciously turning away from our idols. Jesus, though he was without sin, underwent a cleansing baptism before going into the wilderness to be tempted, and so we will do well to submit ourselves afresh to our merciful God and let him wash us clean of the stains of idolatry.

We must also not miss the fact that Jesus triumphed over instant gratification after "He had fasted 40 days and 40 nights" (Matt. 4:2). That is no coincidence. Roy Baumeister, a psychology professor at Florida State University, suggests that "any kind of self-discipline—holding your breath, fasting, writing like a southpaw if you're right-handed—can strengthen willpower."[5]

But fasting, whether from food or other pleasures and necessities, is an especially potent form of self-denial and spiritual discipline and therefore the ideal antidote for the idol of instant gratification. Fasting is a physical, practical way of crucifying "the flesh with its passions and desires" (Gal. 5:24). It is a way to remind our bodies and minds that "our old self was crucified with Christ in order that sin's dominion over the body may be abolished, so that we may no longer be enslaved to sin" (Rom. 6:6). It is a way to "discipline the body and bring it under strict control" (1 Cor. 9:27) in order to win a spiritual victory.

If you are willing to overcome the idol of instant gratification in your life, then in Jesus' name, I call you to a fast. It may be a fast from food or from some other pleasure or necessity. You may undertake it alone, or you may enlist a partner. You may hear God calling you to a specific fast already, or you may choose one of the following ideas:

- Fast from food. There are many ways to do this, of course, and if you have any physical challenges (diabetes or high blood pressure, etc.), you should consult a doctor first. But possibilities include:

  1. Fast one meal a day for a certain length of time (a week, a month, forty days, etc.).

  2. Fast one day a week for a certain length of time.

  3. Fast for more than a day. (If this is your first attempt, you should build up to periods longer than twenty-four hours.)

- Fast from a habit (coffee, for example, or the morning newspaper).
- Fast from external stimuli. (Try to go a certain length of time without television or radio, for example.)
- Fast from a pleasure (such as golf, music, movies, your favorite food, etc.).

- Fast from a comfort (air conditioning, soft chairs, etc.).
- Fast from a convenience (telephone, e-mail, dishwasher, etc.).
- Fast from a "necessity" (driving a car, electricity, etc.).
- Fast from "fast" and "instant" things (fast food, instant mashed potatoes, E-ZPass lanes, etc.).

Obviously these are just ideas, and they are far from exhaustive. But the point isn't creativity; it's discipline that will help subdue your drive for instant gratification and remind you that God is capable of providing for your needs and answering your prayers both now and later.

For that reason it is also a good idea, when fasting, to devote extra time to communion with God. If you're fasting from food, for example, spend mealtimes in prayer and Bible reading. That way you'll not only enjoy the benefit of turning your thoughts and actions away from an idol but also of the added time you spend focusing on the true God.

Let this be your heartfelt prayer:

> *Abba, thank you for showing me that I don't have to be a slave to my passions and least of all to my drive for instant gratification. Please forgive my idolatry, and help me to cast this idol far away from me, even as you continue to show me how the "microwave mentality" shows up in other areas of my life.*
>
> *Help me to return to you with all my heart, with fasting (see Joel 2:12). Enable me to crucify my flesh with its passions and desires (see Gal. 5:24), in order that sin's dominion over my body may be abolished, so that I may no longer be enslaved to sin (see Rom. 6:6). Teach me to discipline my body and bring it under strict control (see 1 Cor. 9:27) in order to worship and serve you fully. And help me to be the kind of person who by constant use of my spiritual muscles trains myself to distinguish between good and evil (see Heb. 5:14), in Jesus' name, amen.*

SEVEN

The Superman Myth

He was virtually unknown. His biggest break before 1978 was being selected to star opposite Katherine Hepburn in the Broadway production, *A Matter of Gravity*. He had portrayed Ben Harper on the television soap opera *Love of Life* and had a bit part as a submarine officer in the disaster film, *Grey Lady Down*.

But in 1978, the relatively unknown actor Christopher Reeve was selected from among two hundred candidates to play the title role in *Superman: The Movie*. The film was a hit, inspiring three sequels and making its star famous. In many ways Superman was more than a role for Christopher Reeve. He seemed to embody the Superman ideal. He was tall (6' 4"). He was handsome. He was athletic. He insisted on doing his own stunts in his films. He earned a pilot's license in his early twenties and twice flew solo across the Atlantic in a small plane. He was an expert sailor, scuba diver, skier, and horseman.

He was flying high, but then he came crashing to earth.

In 1995, he was competing in an equestrian event near Charlottesville, Virginia, when his horse threw him. He landed headfirst, fracturing the uppermost vertebrae in his spine and paralyzing him from the neck down. Suddenly, tragically, he couldn't feel his body. He couldn't move his arms or legs. He couldn't even breathe without assistance.

The man who had personified the Superman myth had been literally thrown from a high horse. As journalist Michael Gove wrote:

> The contrast between the myth of Superman, the sheer potency of this fictional creation, and the eventual fate of Christopher Reeve is inescapably poignant. The actor who played a figure capable of transcending human weakness was, horrifically, trapped by the frailty of his own body. An accident sustained while enjoying his own athletic prowess reduced him to a paralysed state. He became the prisoner of flesh that would no longer respond to his own, indomitable, spirit.[1]

Though he eventually reclaimed the ability to breathe without a respirator for short periods, and through rigorous therapy even regained some sensation and movement, Reeve was a quadriplegic for the rest of his life. He died of heart failure in 2004 at the age of fifty-two.

Superman isn't real. He's a myth. A fable. A comic book character, for crying out loud.

We know that, of course. And yet we fall for it over and over again. We so easily and so frequently believe in a myth that, in many ways, Christopher Reeve personified. And we do more than believe in it; we bow down to it and make it an idol.

It's called humanism, and it's a form of idolatry that is nearly as old as the human race.

A Renaissance State of Mind

Humanism is a way of thinking and living that focuses on human abilities and accomplishments. As a modern philosophy, its roots are in the Renaissance:

The Renaissance began in Italy in the 1300s and, over the course of the next two centuries, spread throughout Europe, lasting through the sixteenth century. The Renaissance was characterized by great strides in literature, learning, art, and architecture. Writers and artists such as Petrarch, Boccaccio, Giotto, and Michelangelo sparked an era of extraordinary human accomplishment. The Renaissance also marked a significant shift in human thought. In contrast to the middle ages (in which the major theme of art, literature, and philosophy was glorifying and serving God), Renaissance artists and thinkers exalted man and his abilities. This shift gave birth to a doctrine called humanism, which stressed human dignity and ability and regarded man as the center of all things, the master of his fate, the captain of his soul.[2]

Humanism rejects the idea that God created the world and believes that the best hope for humanity, collectively and individually, lies in the fruits of human intelligence, energy, and accomplishment. Humanists, rather than looking to God for answers and assistance, look only to themselves and their fellow beings, believing (in the words of psychologist Erich Fromm) "in the perfectibility of man"[3]—that is, humanity's ability to continue improving until wars cease, poverty is eliminated, and unhappiness is a mere memory.

While modern humanism is a philosophy born of the Renaissance, it could be said to have coalesced in 1933, with the signing of "The Humanist Manifesto" (which has been followed by two sequels, The Humanist Manifesto II and The Humanist Manifesto III). Over the course of the twentieth century, humanism became even more widespread than before until it qualifies today as a quintessentially American idol.

But, while it is perhaps more prevalent than ever, it is a form of idolatry that was around long before America became a nation.

Tower of Power

In the earliest days of human history, the civilization of the entire world was concentrated in the area between the Euphrates and Tigris rivers, in what is today called Iraq. Of civilization at that time, the Bible says:

> At one time the whole earth had the same language and vocabulary. As people migrated from the east, they found a valley in the land of Shinar and settled there. They said to each other, "Come, let us make oven-fired bricks." They had brick for stone and asphalt for mortar. And they said, "Come, let us build ourselves a city and a tower with its top in the sky. Let us make a name for ourselves; otherwise, we will be scattered over the face of the earth."
>
> Then the LORD came down to look over the city and the tower that the men were building. The LORD said, "If, as one people all having the same language, they have begun to do this, then nothing they plan to do will be impossible for them. Come, let Us go down there and confuse their language so that they will not understand one another's speech." So the LORD scattered them from there over the face of the earth, and they stopped building the city. Therefore its name is called Babylon, for there the LORD confused the language of the whole earth, and from there the LORD scattered them over the face of the whole earth. (Gen. 11:1–9)

Now there's a lot of fascinating stuff going on in just those few verses from the first book of the Bible, and there are many intriguing avenues of exploration and study. But for our purposes in discussing the idol of humanism, I would like to focus primarily on the people's sentiments as they prepared and began to build what has been known to thousands of generations since as "the Tower of Babel."

Amazingly, I believe we can see in the biblical account of the Tower of Babel the birth of the attitudes and aspirations that we have come to call humanism. Not only that, but I think the Bible's record actually reveals the three central characteristics of this ancient and American idol.

Human Activity

The first thing the people in the plain of Shinar reportedly said to each other was, "Come, let us make oven-fired bricks" (Gen. 11:3).

Perhaps that strikes you as an odd thing to say or, even more so, as an odd thing to record for posterity. "Come, let us make oven-fired bricks." It could hardly be more surprising if Moses had recorded them saying to each other, "Come, let us make ham sandwiches." But there's a reason such sentiments were recorded. Pastor and author Ray Stedman points out:

> Immediately, the inventiveness of [these] people becomes evident. Remember that these were the technicians of humanity—technologically gifted people. Their native inventiveness becomes evident in the way they adapted to the environment in which they lived. . . . They did not find rocks and stones to build with, such as they had in the land where they had previously lived, so they made bricks out of dirt and clay. Later they discovered the process of burning them—first in the sun, and then in a furnace—until they became hard and impermeable brick such as we know it today.
>
> All this is given to us in one sentence in the Bible, but we know from history that it occupied a period of time. Man did not discover all this at one time but learned how to make bricks and later how to burn them. They also lacked lime for cement so could not make mortar, as we know it, but some inventive Yankee among them discovered a tar pit which was filled with natural asphalt (these are common throughout the Middle East). They discovered that the tar was sticky and they used this natural bitumen, this asphalt, for mortar. They had then a substitute for stones and cement. They made bricks and used asphalt for mortar

and thus demonstrated how adaptable they were to the situation they found.[4]

The statement, "Come, let us make oven-fired bricks," is more than necessary groundwork for the rest of the story; it is a central feature of humanism. The ninth thesis of the Humanist Manifesto states, "In the place of the old attitudes involved in worship and prayer the humanist finds his religious emotions expressed in a heightened sense of personal life and in a cooperative effort to promote social well-being."[5] In other words, "If it's going to be, it's up to me." *Human* activity—not God's—is the means by which progress will be made and redemption obtained.

It's the philosophy expressed in John Lennon's song, "Imagine." The song, released in 1971, featured Lennon at what may have been his vocal and lyrical peak. The subtle arrangement and utopian theme combined to make this Lennon's biggest solo hit, as he encouraged people to imagine no hell, no countries, and no religions, which he claimed would create an era of global peace and "a brotherhood of man."[6]

John Lennon was a gifted musician and songwriter, but that song reveals a distinctly humanist philosophy. Humanism says, "Come, let us make oven-fired bricks." "We can do it." "It's easy if you try." But that is an idolatrous attitude. Contrary to biblical faith, which encourages reliance on God, the idol of humanism induces people to bow down to their own efforts and believe that human activity is the answer to all the world's needs.

Human Capability

The second thing the Bible says about these people's intentions is as significant as the first. "Come," they said, "let us build ourselves a city and a tower with its top in the sky" (Gen. 11:4). This statement reveals not only faith in human activity but also an equally misplaced faith in human capability. To quote Ray Stedman again:

They began to talk excitedly about building a city and a tower. The two things they mentioned are very significant, very revealing. The appearance of the first city was back in the story of Cain and Abel, when Cain went out and built a city. It illustrated the hunger of humanity to huddle together for companionship, even though they were not really ready to do it (as they still, obviously, are not ready to live together successfully in cities). God's final intention is to build a city for man. Abraham looked for "a city which has foundations, whose builder and maker is God" (Heb. 11:10 RSV). But man was not yet ready for that. Now here they are, again ready to build a city to satisfy the desires of body and soul. There is nothing that does this better than for human beings to live together in cities. Cities are centers of commercial and business life where all the needs of the body can best be met. Also, cities are centers of pleasure and culture, where all the hungers of the soul can be satisfied: hunger for beauty, art, and music and all the ingredients of culture. The tower, on the other hand, is designed to satisfy the spirit of man. Here we see, reflected in these two things, a fundamental understanding of the nature of man as body, soul, and spirit. All are to be satisfied in these two elementary needs, the city and the tower.

A number of years ago, digging in the plains of Shinar, archaeologists discovered the remains of certain great towers that these early Babylonians had built. Some archaeologists have felt that they may even have found the foundation of this original tower of Babel. That is very hard to determine. But they did find that the Babylonians built great towers called *ziggurats*, which were built in a circular fashion with an ascending staircase that terminates in a shrine at the top, around which are written the signs of the zodiac. Obviously, the tower was a religious building, intending to expose man to the mystery of the heavens and the greatness of God. That, perhaps, is what is meant here by the statement that they intended to build a tower with its top in the heavens. They were impressed by its greatness architecturally, that is, it was a colossal thing for the men

of that day to build and they may have thus thought of
it as reaching into heaven.[7]

It is a mistake to believe that the people's intention in building this tower was to communicate with God. The next sentence
reveals that God was the furthest thing from their minds. They
were enamored by their own abilities. Their new technology
opened new vistas to them. They believed, literally, that "the sky
was the limit." They were excited to "boldly go where no man has
gone before."

As in ancient times, so it is in our day. The Humanist
Manifesto II declared:

> Dramatic scientific, technological, and ever-accelerating
> social and political changes crowd our awareness. We
> have virtually conquered the planet, explored the moon,
> overcome the natural limits of travel and communica-
> tion; we stand at the dawn of a new age, ready to move
> farther into space and perhaps inhabit other planets.
> Using technology wisely, we can control our environ-
> ment, conquer poverty, markedly reduce disease, extend
> our life-span, significantly modify our behavior, alter the
> course of human evolution and cultural development,
> unlock vast new powers, and provide humankind with
> unparalleled opportunity for achieving an abundant and
> meaningful life.[8]

Those who place their faith in human capability are bowing to
an idol. As the psalmist once sang:

> A king is not saved by a large army;
>   a warrior will not be delivered by great strength.
> The horse is a false hope for safety;
>   it provides no escape by its great power.
> [But] the eye of the LORD is on those who fear Him—
>   those who depend on His faithful love
> to deliver them from death
>   and to keep them alive in famine.
> We wait for the LORD;
>   He is our help and our shield. (Ps. 33:16–20)

Human Glory

The final statement of the people who lived in the plains of Shinar is perhaps the most revealing. Three times the Bible account quotes them as saying, "Let us . . ." Each statement becomes ever more blatant, more revealing into the true attitudes of their hearts.

The third and final word we hear from these proto-humanists is, "Let us make a name for ourselves; otherwise, we will be scattered over the face of the whole earth" (Gen. 11:4). Rather than seeking God's glory, they determined to seek their own. Not only that, but they clearly intended this city and this tower as a means of contravening God's command to "spread out over the earth and multiply on it" (Gen. 9:7). They were unconcerned both with God's plan and with God's glory. As Ray Stedman says:

> "The ultimate motive is expressed in these words, 'let us make a name for ourselves.'"
>
> From that day on, this has been the motto of humanity, "let us make a name for ourselves." I am always amused to see how many public edifices make a plaque somewhere on which the names of all the public officials who were in power when it was built are inscribed: the mayor, the head of public works, etc. "Let us make a name for ourselves," is a fundamental urge of a fallen race. It reveals one of the basic philosophies of humanism: "Glory to man in the highest, for man is the master of things." That is the central thought of humanism, glory to mankind.[9]

With the words, "Let us make a name for ourselves," the people's idolatry becomes clear. Rather than seeking God's face, they are intent on erecting a monument to themselves. Instead of bowing in his glorious presence, they seek glory for themselves. Instead of following God's plan for their lives, they boldly walk in the opposite direction. They choose idolatry.

Perhaps God was remembering such rebellion when, years later, he spoke through Moses to the vast nation he had delivered out of slavery in Egypt:

> "Be careful that you don't forget the LORD your God by
> failing to keep His command—the ordinances and
> statutes—I am giving you today. When you eat and are
> full, and build beautiful houses to live in, and your herds
> and flocks grow large, and your silver and gold multiply,
> and everything else you have increases, be careful that
> your heart doesn't become proud and you forget the
> LORD your God who brought you out of the land of
> Egypt, out of the place of slavery. . . . You may say to
> yourself, 'My power and my own ability have gained this
> wealth for me,' but remember that the LORD your God
> gives you the power to gain wealth, in order to confirm
> His covenant He swore to your fathers, as it is today. If
> you ever forget the LORD your God and go after other
> gods to worship and bow down to them, I testify against
> you today that you will perish." (Deut. 8:11–14, 17–19)

The heart that forgets God and instead bows before human activity, capability, and glory is an idolatrous heart and one that is destined to reap the results of such idolatry: confusion and division.

Ball of Confusion

Idolatry always leads to destruction. The Bible records the inevitable fate of those who exalt the idol of humanism:

> Then the LORD came down to look over the city and the
> tower that the men were building. The LORD said, "If,
> as one people all having the same language, they have
> begun to do this, then nothing they plan to do will be
> impossible for them. Come, let Us go down there and
> confuse their language so that they will not understand
> one another's speech." So the LORD scattered them
> from there over the face of the earth, and they stopped
> building the city. Therefore its name is called Babylon.
> (Gen. 11:5–9)

The text says, "The Lord came down to look over the city and the tower." That is not an indication that God needed information. He did not need to discover what had been happening. He never needs to learn anything because "nothing in all creation is hidden from God's sight" (Heb. 4:13 NIV). No, the language the biblical author uses in this passage is not intended to depict a God who needs information; it was written this way to convey something else entirely. Stedman explains:

> I know that in certain circles the idea of a God who comes down to visit earth is regarded as an expression of a primitive concept of God—that God lives up in heaven somewhere but is cut off from direct communication from earth and is dependent upon certain messenger boys who travel back and forth to keep him informed. Somehow a message reaches God about man's tower and he decides to come down and investigate. But this language is not a primitive concept of God. It is impossible to read it that way if you read it in the light of what has already been said about God in the book of Genesis. Already God has been presented as the maker of heaven and earth, the One concerned about the minutest details of creation, the Omnipotent, Omniscient God who knows everything, sees everything and is all-powerful.
>
> No, this is not a primitive concept of God at all; it is an ironic expression. It is a humorous expression, if you please, designed to indicate to us, in a very clever way, the ridiculousness of this whole situation. Here is this tower that men erect, thinking that it will take God's breath away, it will threaten him. Men think, "Here we are, we wild Promethean creatures; we've dared to invade the heavens! You had better watch out, God!" But up in the real heavens this tower is so little that God can't see it. It is so tiny that even the strongest telescope in heaven does not reveal it. So God says, "I'll come down and investigate." It is language designed to set in contrast the ridiculousness of the suppositions of men, and the greatness of the Being of God. He "came down" to investigate this tiny tower that men had erected.[10]

The narrative continues, with God saying next, "If, as one people all having the same language, they have begun to do this, then nothing they plan to do will be impossible for them."

Doesn't that seem strange? Doesn't God seem to be saying the same thing the people themselves are saying? Isn't he acknowledging their tremendous abilities and potential? Yes. Absolutely. He created them that way, didn't he? He made human beings "a little lower than the heavenly beings and crowned [them] with glory and honor" (Ps. 8:5 NIV). He knew better than they did just how far their potential extended. But it was a potential he intended for his glory, not theirs.

What happens next is important. It's easy to misunderstand God's words and actions, but once they are understood, they open the door to some profound truths. God continues speaking, and he says, "Come, let Us go down there and confuse their language so that they will not understand one another's speech" (Gen. 11:7).

The first thing to emphasize in that short verse is the first three words: "Come, let Us." Those sound familiar, don't they? They are the very words the people used to express their idolatrous ambitions:

- "Come, let us make oven-fired bricks" (v. 3).
- "Come, let us build ourselves a city and a tower" (v. 4).
- "Let us make a name for ourselves" (v. 4).

Three times the people said, "Let us do this or that." But God responded "Come, let *Us.*" Just once. It is another intimation of his mighty power in contrast to their human efforts. He speaks once and reverses all their idolatrous intentions. Not in anger. Not in vengeance. I believe even those words were spoken lovingly. I believe they were the words of a God who knew far better than they the destructiveness of idols. God said, in effect, "Let us go down and confuse their language, for their sake, to protect them from themselves, to stop their sinful folly, which can result only in the misery of separation from me and all the good things I have planned for them."

The Best-Laid Plans

But we are not like the people who lived in the land of Shinar, right? We do not bow to the idol of humanism. We know better. Except on those days when we don't feel the need to seek God in prayer and cry out for his help, figuring we're equal to whatever tasks lie ahead without his intervention. Or when we comb through books and manuals for human wisdom rather than diligently studying the word of truth to draw upon God's wisdom (2 Tim. 2:15).

Except for those times when we rely on our own cleverness or capabilities in a meeting. Or run ahead of God, believing that our activity is more important than his approval. Or when we willfully disobey God's clear command.

Except for those tendencies we have to tell ourselves (or our children), "You can do it!" instead of "I am able to do all things through Him who strengthens me" (Phil. 4:13). Or "Where there's a will, there's a way," instead of "God will make a way." Or "mind over matter," instead of "When I am weak, then I am strong" (2 Cor. 12:10).

Except for those occasions when we try to do God's work in our own power. When we act as though the church exists to meet our needs, instead of providing us a place of ministry, mission, and service. When we try to build our own little kingdoms instead of playing our part in extending God's kingdom.

Except for those moments when we neglect the opportunity to give glory to God. When we accept, or invite, praise that belongs to him alone. When we reject vulnerability and accountability (refusing to confess our sins to one another [James 5:16]) because we prefer to "make a name" for ourselves. When we let others place us on a pedestal.

I mention such things not to produce condemnation; there is no condemnation for those who are in Christ Jesus (Rom. 8:1). But if any of the previous paragraphs shine a light not on exceptions or occasional failings but on a pattern of life, they may indicate the degree to which the idol of humanism has infiltrated your heart and life. In fact, if you would open the door of your heart wider to God's will and work, take a few moments to read over the above paragraphs, asking the Holy Spirit to convict you of sin or release you if your heart is free of such idolatry.

Confounding the Superman Myth

"So the LORD scattered them from there over the face of the earth" (Gen. 11:8), the account ends. Isn't it amazing that this story began with the people building a great city and tower so they wouldn't be scattered over the face of the earth, and it ends with them being scattered over the face of the earth? "The best-laid plans of mice and men," said Robert Burns, "often go awry." Idol worship never takes us where we want to go; it always ends up in disappointment and destruction.

Happily, however, just as God halted their humanistic ambitions and cast down their idolatrous tower, he can also cast down the idol of humanism in your life and save you from its control and consequences in your life.

For that to happen, of course, you must admit your idolatry and repent of it, taking words with you, as Hosea says (Hos. 14:2). Having done that, let me suggest a spiritual exercise that may help you, with the Holy Spirit's help, cast the idol of humanism far from your heart and life. I suggest that you employ this practice for as long as you think is necessary, whether that is a week, a month, or even for the rest of your life. If humanistic beliefs and behaviors are deeply ingrained within you, continue this exercise until you no longer habitually put faith in human activity, rely on your own capability, and seek the glory of anyone but the Lord your God.

It's a simple but strikingly uncommon practice. At least once a day prostrate yourself before the God of heaven and earth. In other words, lie down flat on your face on the floor and touch your forehead to the ground. Go as low as you can get. As you lower yourself, pour out praises to God. Give him honor and glory. Tell him (and remind yourself) that you are prostrating yourself before him because he is God and you are not. You don't have to do or say anything fancy; a simple, repeated phrase like, "God, I bow before you," or "Almighty God, I humble myself in your presence, I praise you, and I worship you" may be all you need to say. If you feel the need to say more, you might want to read a psalm aloud in this position (see Psalm 8; 19; 44; 63; 90).

You may wish to spend five minutes or fifteen minutes in this exercise, but you should do it daily for at least a week—longer if you think it necessary. You may decide to make it a part of your daily prayer practice. You may want to return to it periodically (every Saturday, for example, or for the season of Lent).

If you find it hard to do this, don't give up. If you miss a day or more, keep at it. If you struggle with this exercise, it may be an indication of just how deeply rooted this American idol has become in your life. Don't be discouraged. Jesus has overcome the whole world (John 16:33); he can overcome this idol in your heart.

> *God, you created the heavens and the earth. You created me. You are God. You are my God. I bow before you. I worship you. I exalt you and glorify you above all.*
>
> *Forgive me for ever bowing to the idol of humanism. Forgive me for ever thinking that I can accomplish anything apart from you. You are the vine, and I am the branch; apart from you I can do nothing.*
>
> *Thank you for all your good gifts to me. Save me from the idolatry of forgetting you and thinking that my own power and my own ability have gotten those things for me. You give me the power to gain wealth and to accomplish great things. You have promised that I can do even greater things than Jesus did on this earth but only if I trust in you and rely on you moment by moment.*
>
> *Teach me, Lord God, that it is not by might nor by power but by your Spirit (see Zech. 4:6) that I do anything, in Jesus' name, amen.*

EIGHT

The Cult of Personal Experience

I know a man named Stan. Stan loves God and follows Jesus. I've never had a conversation with him that didn't revolve around spiritual things.

But for the longest time I avoided him. When conversation was unavoidable, I would make it as short as possible. When I couldn't get away quickly, I would fervently pray for deliverance.

This bothered me. I wasn't sure why. But I think I figured it out recently. It's not that Stan wasn't a dear Christian brother. It's not that he has ever done anything to offend me. It's simply this: Stan is a cultist.

Now, don't get me wrong. He's not into Hare Krishna or the Worldwide Church of the Holy Flaming Sword of Spock. That's not what I mean. I mean, he's immersed in the cult of personal experience.

Every time I see him, he tells me excitedly about this "faith healer" or that "prophet" he's just encountered or this conference or that revival where he's just witnessed a new outbreak of spiritual power. He has told me stories of incredible healings he has witnessed and amazing displays of God's power he has seen. Every time I see him, it seems he's just returned from a different city with a new CD to lend to me (and meanwhile, the several different churches he attends are desperate for nursery workers, Sunday school teachers, and other volunteers).

The Moving Springs in All the Affairs of Life

Stan is not unique. I've encountered many such folks who bow at the altar of personal experience. I've done so myself.

Our culture and churches today are filled with people who are looking for an emotionally fulfilling experience. And there's nothing wrong with that. On the contrary, it's wonderful that churches throughout North America have experienced a revival of sorts in our forms of worship, largely through music and other means that connect the worshipper's head *and* heart with a transcendent, awesome God. In many churches over the past few decades, worship had become an exercise in endurance, a cold and dry experience. People hungered, as they should, for worship that engages the emotions as well as the intellect.

This is nothing new. Jonathan Edwards, a prominent preacher and theologian of the Great Awakening that swept America in the mid-eighteenth century, defended the role of personal experience in the spiritual life, saying that the emotions are "the moving springs in all the affairs of life." He wrote: "I am bold to assert, that there was never any considerable change wrought in the mind or conversions of any person, by any thing of religious nature that ever he read, heard, or saw, who had not his affections moved."[1]

It is not idolatrous at all to seek God with all your heart and mind and soul. It is not idolatrous at all to hunger for an experiential encounter with God. It becomes idolatry, however, when we lapse into the error of Simon Magus, as recorded in the book of Acts.

Simon's Surprise

In the earliest years of the church, after Jesus had ascended to heaven and the church in Jerusalem had received the Holy Spirit and begun to grow dramatically, a period of persecution followed. Saul of Tarsus had been given authority by the religious leaders in Jerusalem to hunt down these followers of Jesus and drag them off into prison (Acts 8:3).

With so much persecution going on in Jerusalem, the churches went underground, and many Christ followers took their message elsewhere. A man named Philip was one such person:

> Philip went down to a city in Samaria and preached the Messiah to them. The crowds paid attention with one mind to what Philip said, as they heard and saw the signs he was performing. For unclean spirits, crying out with a loud voice, came out of many who were possessed, and many who were paralyzed and lame were healed. So there was great joy in that city. (Acts 8:5–8)

There was a man named Simon in that city, who "had previously practiced sorcery . . . and astounded the Samaritan people, while claiming to be somebody great" (Acts 8:9). This sorcerer's magic and magnetism had gained him fame and, it may safely be supposed, fortune as well.

> But when [the Samaritan people] believed Philip, as he proclaimed the good news about the kingdom of God and the name of Jesus Christ, both men and women were baptized. Then even Simon himself believed. And after he was baptized, he went around constantly with Philip and was astounded as he observed the signs and great miracles that were being performed. (Acts 8:12–13)

Simon, the famous magician, "believed," "was baptized," and became a disciple, following Philip everywhere he went. And this former charlatan and new Christ follower was astounded as he observed healings and exorcisms in the name of Jesus. We may imagine that, while he knew every trick of the trade when it came to illusion and the dark arts, it was something else entirely to see authentic miracles being performed in the power of the Holy Spirit.

But for all that, Simon's surprise was just beginning.

Simon Says

Simon the magician may have been the most prominent person in Samaria to convert to the new Christian faith, but he was far from the only one. Many people followed Jesus as a result of Philip's ministry. So, when the apostles in Jerusalem heard that even Samaritans were believing in Jesus the Messiah, they sent Peter and John to join Philip.

> After [Peter and John] went down there, they prayed for
> [the Samaritans], that they might receive the Holy
> Spirit. For He had not yet come down on any of them;
> they had only been baptized in the name of the Lord
> Jesus. Then Peter and John laid their hands on them,
> and they received the Holy Spirit. (Acts 8:15–17)

The Bible doesn't specify what sorts of signs or manifestations accompanied this Samaritan Pentecost. But, if it was like the Pentecost in Jerusalem, the giving of the Spirit came with the sound of a "violent rushing wind," "tongues, like flames of fire that were divided [and] rested on each one of them," and a miraculous ability to speak in other languages, "as the Spirit gave them ability for speech" (see Acts 2:2–4). It's apparent that something like that happened because Simon—who had already seen Philip performing miracles—freaked out, so to speak:

> When Simon saw that the Holy Spirit was given through
> the laying on of the apostles' hands, he offered them
> money, saying, "Give me this power too, so that anyone
> I lay hands on may receive the Holy Spirit."
> But Peter told him, "May your silver be destroyed
> with you, because you thought the gift of God could be

obtained with money! You have no part or share in this
matter, because your heart is not right before God.
Therefore repent of this wickedness of yours, and pray
to the Lord that the intent of your heart may be for-
given you. For I see you are poisoned by bitterness and
bound by iniquity."

"Please pray to the Lord for me," Simon replied,
"so that nothing you have said may happen to me."

Then, after they had testified and spoken the mes-
sage of the Lord, they [Peter and John] traveled back to
Jerusalem, evangelizing many villages of the Samaritans.
(Acts 8:18–25)

Strong Medicine

Peter's words to Simon seem pretty harsh, if you ask me.
Maybe the guy wasn't too smart, but he was just asking for more
spiritual power; it's not like he committed any great sin, right?
Wrong.

Peter's response makes clear that Simon's offense was serious.
As Lloyd J. Ogilvie has written, this was "strong spiritual medicine for a false medicine man to take."[2] But it wasn't for his words
alone that Peter rebuked Simon; it was for the idolatrous "intent
of [his] heart" (Acts 8:22).

Simon, though he had believed, been baptized, and set out to
follow Jesus, nonetheless fell quickly and easily into idolatry. He
saw what the apostles had. He coveted their spiritual power and
authority. And from his example we can draw an outline of the
cult of personal experience. We can discover what it means to
exalt our experience—even a "Christian" experience—to a position that displaces God. And we can also learn how to halt and
overcome that subtle form of idolatry in our own lives.

An Idolatrous Motive

I believe that we can see in the story of Simon Magus, the
motive that lies at the root, below the surface, of the cult of

personal experience. When this former magician saw what happened when Peter and John laid their hands on the new believers in Samaria and prayed for them to receive the Holy Spirit, he apparently felt a desire arise within him. He apparently had no idea it was a sinful desire. He apparently had no clue that the coming of the Spirit to the Samaritans had prompted in him not godly worship but idolatry. But his first words should have given him an indication. Do you remember what his first words were? "When Simon saw that the Holy Spirit was given through the laying on of the apostles' hands, he offered them money, saying, *'Give me*, . . .' " (Acts 8:18a, italics added).

Give me. Simon said "me." In so many words, he revealed that his motive was idolatrous. The cult of personal experience is idolatrous—even when it seems to be seeking spiritual, even Christian, things—because it is self-centered. This is nowhere more evident than in our worship lives as Christ followers.

True worship focuses on God. Idolatrous worship focuses on me. A true worshipper says, like Jesus, "I seek not to please myself but him who sent me" (John 5:30 NIV). Someone who is immersed in the cult of personal experience sounds more like the Spice Girls: "Give me what I want, what I really, really want." *LOL*

When the motive in worship is meeting *my* needs—as if I'm saying to the worship leaders, the preacher, and the other participants, "OK, move *me!* Thrill *me!* Bless *me!*"—then I, like Simon Magus, am committing idolatry.

John Ortberg and Pam Howell, writing in *Leadership Journal,* hit the nail on the head when they say:

> Can you imagine the Israelites, freshly delivered from slavery, before a mountain that trembles violently with the presence of God (Exod. 19), muttering: "We're leaving because we're not singing the songs we like. Like that tambourine song, how come they don't do that tambourine song anymore?"
>
> "I don't like it when Moses leads worship—Aaron's better."

"This is too formal—all that smoke and mystery.
I like casual worship."
"It was OK, except for Miriam's dance—too wild,
not enough reverence. And I don't like the tambourine."[3]

Scripture doesn't read like that, does it? Why not? Because it is idolatry to focus on "What am *I* getting out of worship?" That is the wrong question. If we are worshippers, and not idolaters, we will ask ourselves, "What is *God* getting out of my worship?" As the Westminster Confession puts it, "The chief end of man is to glorify God and enjoy him forever," *not* the other way around.

Marva Dawn, in her book *Reaching Out without Dumbing Down*, remarks "how difficult it is to keep God as the subject of worship in [our] present narcissistic and subjectivized culture."[4]

Yet the paradox is this: the only personally fulfilling worship is worship that doesn't seek personal fulfillment! The only personally fulfilling experience is one that isn't focused on personal fulfillment. The only personally fulfilling *life* is one that is God-centered rather than self-centered.

As E. Stanley Jones says:

> What brings pleasure? The pursuit of pleasure itself? There must be an emphatic, No! Pleasure and happiness are by-products. Pursue them as ends in themselves, and they will rot in your hands. . . . The pleasure principle only works when it is linked to something beyond itself. It comes as a by-product of service to God and man.[5]

Those who seek their own pleasure will go away empty; those who seek God's pleasure will be filled (see Matt. 5:6). "Give me" is the language of idolatry; "Give to the LORD" (Ps. 29:2 *God's Word*) is the language of worship.

An Idolatrous Focus

We can see in the story of Simon Magus not only an idolatrous motive but also an idolatrous focus. Look at the account again:

> When Simon saw that the Holy Spirit was given through
> the laying on of the apostles' hands, he offered them
> money, saying, "Give me *this power.*" (Acts 8:18–19,
> italics added)

Simon's words reveal another facet to the cult of personal
experience and another challenge to the ways we worship and live
our lives. Notice that he offered Peter and John money and said,
"Give me this ability." Though he was surely impressed by the
manifestations of the Holy Spirit—the sound of a rushing, mighty
wind, perhaps, or people speaking in languages they had not previously known—he was most impressed that it happened when
the apostles laid their hands on the believers. And Simon wanted
that power.

Preacher and scholar Matthew Henry wrote of Simon:

> He was ambitious to have the honour of an apostle, but
> not at all solicitous to have the spirit of a Christian. He
> was more desirous to gain honour to himself than to do
> good to others.[6]

That is certainly true, but this seems much more to the point: he
sought the gift not the Giver.

This is the central idolatry of the cult of personal experience.
This is the great sin of those among us who "according to their
own desires . . . accumulate teachers for themselves because they
have an itch to hear something new" (2 Tim. 4:3). This is the
error of those whose worship is warped by frantically seeking this
gift or that, instead of enjoying the presence of God in whatever
way he may choose to show himself. This is the difference in those
who bow to the idol of personal experience.

We long more fervently for an ecstatic experience than for the
One who comes, sometimes in whirlwinds and sometimes in a
still, small voice. We seek a rush of emotion more than we do God
himself. We seek the gift and not the Giver.

However, when we take our focus off the experience—whether
the style of the service, our own preferences, the expectation of a

[handwritten marginal notes, partially legible:] The sermon @ Ebenezer B... in 1953 and appalled that 11:00 on Sunday morning is the most segregated hour in Christian America "Damascus"

certain kind of blessing—then we are turning away from idolatry and moving closer to God himself. That is why the spiritually mature person can worship to the tune of a guitar *or* a pipe organ. The true worshipper can turn the words of the most ancient creed *and* the simplest chorus into an act of worship. The man or woman after God's heart can worship through liturgy or through a children's sermon. This doesn't mean we may not have preferences, nor does it mean that the quality and content of a worship service don't matter; but I do mean to say that true worship doesn't require a certain style or a favorite song unless we are seeking an experience or a gift more than the Giver.

An Idolatrous Result

The final part of Simon's experience that I think we can learn from is found in Peter's statement, in verses 20–23:

> But Peter told him, "May your silver be destroyed with you, because you thought the gift of God could be obtained with money! You have no part or share in this matter, because your heart is not right before God. Therefore repent of this wickedness of yours, and pray to the Lord that the intent of your heart may be forgiven you. For I see you are poisoned by bitterness and bound by iniquity." (Acts 8:20–23)

"You are poisoned by bitterness and bound by iniquity," Peter said. He referred to Simon's attitude as "wickedness." Lloyd Ogilvie elaborates:

> Peter used a very potent word in confronting Simon with his spiritual imperiousness and desire to get and control the Spirit—"wickedness," *poneria* in Greek, meaning compulsive determination to continue in a direction we know is wrong. It is sin which becomes so much the focus of the will that we no longer desire to change it and want God to approve it and bless us anyway. Another way of saying that is: we want the Lord on our own terms without surrender of our volitional determination to run our own lives.[7]

That, of course, is the essence of idolatry, for when we make our experience a god, we have effectively replaced God in our affections. And the result is, and will always be, the end of idolatry: bitterness and wickedness.

Oh, my friend, if as you read this chapter God is speaking to your heart and convicting you of the idolatry of devotion not to him but to an idol, the cult of personal experience, I plead with you not to ignore the Spirit's voice. Don't make the mistake of continuing in a direction you know is wrong and expecting God to approve it and bless you anyway. Stop where you are and turn around.

The Turning

Simon's response to Peter's rebuke is pretty much the end of the story, as Luke recorded it in Acts: "Please pray to the Lord for me," Simon replied, "so that nothing you have said may happen to me" (Acts 8:24).

It ends there rather abruptly. The next verse simply tells of the apostles returning to Jerusalem, ministering on the way. It doesn't say that Simon was restored. It doesn't say he continued to go around constantly with Philip, as he had done before (Acts 8:13). It doesn't say that he departed from the faith. But the account may give us a clue, as Ogilvie explains:

> [Simon] completely sidestepped [Peter's] challenge to repent. He asked Peter to pray that none of the things with which he confronted him would happen, but he did not do the one thing which could prevent it—repent! Simon was still in charge of Simon, and he received neither the initial blessing Philip preached nor the fullness of the blessing Peter and John offered. He was left with the same old Simon and a city which no longer was impressed by his assertions of greatness.[8]

Later Christian writers such as Justin Martyr give us some reason to believe that Simon did not repent but instead turned even more effectively to magic and deception. They suggest that he even took his heresy to Rome, the capital of the empire, and became so famous as to have a statue erected in Rome, honoring him as a god.

It's tragic. He could have turned and received forgiveness and grace if he had only done what Peter urged and not only prayed to escape the consequences of his idolatry but repented of the idolatry itself. There is a lesson even in that.

Some whom the Spirit convicts of the cult of personal experience will, like Simon, experience regret when they realize the danger into which they've drifted. But if, like Simon, they seek only to escape the dangers, their search will progress as it began: in selfishness.

But if you believe that God's Holy Spirit has confronted you with "the intent of your heart" (Acts 8:22) and revealed to you that your spiritual life and Christian walk have been poisoned by an emphasis on experience instead of seeking first God and his kingdom, consider the words of Oswald Chambers:

> Is Jesus Christ the Lord of your experiences, or do you place your experiences above Him? Is any experience dearer to you than your Lord? You must allow Him to be Lord over you, and pay no attention to any experience over which He is not Lord. Then there will come a time when God will make you impatient with your own experience, and you can truthfully say, "I do not care what I experience—I am sure of Him!"
>
> Be relentless and hard on yourself if you are in the habit of talking about the experiences you have had.[9]

Be relentless with yourself. Search your heart. Turn your face to God. Don't seek simply a different experience. Don't seek only the gift of God, even forgiveness itself. Seek *him*. Seek his desires. Seek to make his heart happy with the response of your heart.

If you're not quite sure how to do that, maybe a prayer like the following will help:

*Lord, I confess that I have been chasing after an idol.
I have been worshipping at the altar of personal experience.
I have been seeking the gift instead of the Giver.
    I'm not sure I even know how, Lord, but I ask
for your help in turning away from my self-centered, self-
aggrandizing, self-seeking ways. I repent. I turn from
those intentions as much as I know how right now.
    I'm not even sure I know how to seek you and you
alone. But I want to want to. I desire to desire you. It
would please me to please you. Teach me what that means,
and help me to experience your forgiveness, grace, and
goodness not for my pleasure but for yours (knowing, even
as I pray, that when I find pleasure in pleasing you, all
other pleasures and pursuits will grow strangely dim), in
Jesus' name, amen.*

If you have prayed that prayer, you have begun the process of casting down the idol of personal experience in your life. But that is not all you can do. Let me suggest another exercise, one that you may repeat daily (or several times daily) or weekly, to help you be transformed by renewing your mind (Rom. 12:2).

Habakkuk was a prophet who lived during the time of Jeremiah and probably wrote in the years before the Babylonians invaded Judah and took many Jews into captivity. He may have written the last part of his book before the temple in Jerusalem was destroyed—or after. In any case, its final verses are the testimony of a heart that is determined not to depend on circumstances or experience for fulfillment but to be faithful and to seek God apart from ecstatic (or even endurable) experiences.

Consider this, then: Print Habakkuk 3:17–18 on an index card and keep it in your purse, pocket, or Bible, or on your bathroom mirror. Say it aloud at least once a week (more, if you prefer), to remind your heart and mind that God seeks your love, worship, and obedience both through your experience and in spite of it.

Father God, I want to believe in you when I feel like it and when I don't. I want to love you when times are good and when times are bad. I want to triumph in you when the fig tree buds and when there is no fruit at all on the vine. I want to rejoice in you even when the crop fails and there are no sheep in the pen, no cattle in the stall, and no money in the bank. I want to worship you not primarily to bring pleasure to me, but to give pleasure to you and to give the glory that is due your name (see Ps. 29:2).

Deliver me from the cult of personal experience, and help me to learn anew how to worship you and enjoy you forever, in Jesus' name, amen.

NINE

The Lexus
Nexus

He has limousines.
Helicopters.

A yacht.

A Manhattan penthouse.

An "empire of casinos, golf resorts and Manhattan high-rise buildings."[1]

Best-selling books.

A parade of wives who are much younger (and much, much prettier) than him.

His own beauty pageant.

A hit television show.

Fawning admirers. Thousands of employees. Millions of dollars.

It's good to be Donald Trump (despite the hideous hairstyle). But it's not just his wealth that appeals to us; it's the golden patina of success. While he has certainly (and publicly) had his failures, he seems to rise as high and live as large as the big-city skyscrapers he has built and bought and sold.

We watch and read and hear such tales of success with fascination. And we also pursue success—even worship it—with dedication.

The American Dream

"The American Dream," writes journalist Marshall Allen, "is one of the greatest things about the United States. This is a country where anyone, regardless of race, religion, or economic status, has a chance to become wealthy and powerful."[2] That's a wonderful thing. It's one of the things that has made our nation great and produced such success stories as author Horatio Alger, oil magnate John D. Rockefeller, scientist educator Booker T. Washington, and attorney general Alberto Gonzalez.

But this American dream of success can also be dangerous and detrimental to those of us who follow Jesus Christ. Allen continues:

> It's so ingrained in our cultural DNA that we're easily dissatisfied if we don't achieve riches, power, or even our more humble goals of material security. Plus, we have no finish line when we pursue the American Dream. There's no clear marker that tells us, "Enough is enough. You're successful and secure now. Be content." So we run like hamsters on a wire wheel, always striving for worldly progress—sometimes making it—but never feeling like we've achieved enough. We become worriers, obsessing about our academic standing, our salary, our investment portfolio as if any setback would destroy our dreams and expectations. We fail to appreciate God's provision or experience the "peace that surpasses all understanding" that the Bible promises us because we're gluttons who always want more. In times like these, the American Dream is detrimental to our faith because we've made it—often subconsciously—into an idol. It's something we're pursuing instead of God.[3]

Even when it's not something we're pursuing instead of God, it is often something we're pursuing *ahead* of God, which is much the same thing. When a pagan altar in Damascus caught the eye of King Ahaz (2 Kings 16:10–16), he had the priest of God make a copy and place it in the temple. He didn't have the bronze altar, the altar of God's house, moved out of the temple. He simply had it moved aside, and placed the new altar in the temple too.

We do the same, often, with the American dream, the pursuit of success. We don't necessarily forget God or stop worshipping him; we simply move him aside. After all, we still love God; it's just that we have no energy left for prayer after a long day of important meetings. We can't commit to a ministry in our church because of the extra hours we must put in at the office if we hope to get that promotion. Our giving has taken a hit this year because of the payments on the Lexus, but God understands. We may be pursuing our dreams of success *instead* of God, or merely putting them *ahead* of him.

Turning Success into Failure

Like most American idols, there's nothing intrinsically wrong with success. Many successful people have been faithful servants of God. Abraham became so wealthy he and his nephew had to divide the family business. Joseph attained viceroy status in Egypt. David parlayed a cheese-delivery business into a giant-killing enterprise. And Ruth the Moabitess married into money.

God commands us, "Whatever you do, do it enthusiastically" (Col. 3:23). A job well done and a life well lived can bring glory to God. Author Tony Campolo has noted in his book *The Success Fantasy*:

> It is not necessary to be a failure in order to be a fol-
> lower of Jesus. Successful people are also called to follow
> after the Master. The Scripture teaches that those hold-
> ing trophies of success must be willing to lay them at the
> foot of the Cross, willingly surrendering their wealth,
> power, and prestige to Jesus.[4]

But for most of us, it's not past success that presents a prob-lem; it's the pursuit of future success. Whether you're a student striving for straight *A*s, a businessperson hoping for a promotion, an investor looking to make a killing, or a pastor leading a growing church, the drive for success can easily become a fatal flaw. Just ask James and John, the sons of Zebedee.

James and John were two of Jesus' closest friends on earth. He knew them from way back, and they were among the first, and the most enthusiastic, men to enlist in Jesus' ministry. So it only seemed natural for them to seek advancement in his ministry. After all, Jesus was performing miracles, gaining popularity, and acquiring new devotees at a rapid pace. Soon, they felt confident, he would restore the kingdom to the Jewish people and become their king not only spiritually but physically and politically as well.

In anticipation the two brothers decided to strike while the iron was hot. The early bird gets the worm, they figured. God helps those who help themselves, so there was no time like the present (is that enough clichés?):

> Then James and John, the sons of Zebedee, approached [Jesus] and said, "Teacher, we want You to do something for us if we ask You."
>
> "What do you want Me to do for you?" He asked them.
>
> They answered Him, "Allow us to sit at Your right and at Your left in Your glory."
>
> But Jesus said to them, "You don't know what you're asking. Are you able to drink the cup I drink or to be baptized with the baptism I am baptized with?"
>
> "We are able," they told him.
>
> Jesus said to them, "You will drink the cup I drink, and you will be baptized with the baptism I am baptized with. But to sit at My right or left is not Mine to give; instead, it is for those it has been prepared for." When the other 10 disciples heard this, they began to be indignant with James and John. (Mark 10:35–41)

Their plan didn't turn out so well, did it? They took what they thought would be the path to success, and instead they ended up being disappointed and alienating the others in their small band of brothers. That's because they fell victim to the vortex of success, the Lexus Nexus.

A False Assessment of Success

It's easy to look at James's and John's appeal as a transparent, selfish power grab. From the beginning of the story, they look bad. They sound like children:

- "I want to ask you something, but you have to promise to say yes," they say.
- When Jesus asks them what they want, they say, "Can we be first? We want to be first."
- And when he asks them, "Do you think you can drink the cup I must drink?" they respond, "We can, we really can, we promise!"

But more than anything else, their exchange reveals what is wrong with our drive for success: it is based on a false assessment of what success is, what it means. To James and John success meant status, power, position, and recognition. That is the language of this world. But it is not the language of God's kingdom.

We succumb to the idolatry of success-seeking because we believe the world's assessment of what it means to be successful. As Tony Campolo says:

> We all play for prestige. Clergymen seek honorary degrees to write after their names. High school boys pay a high price to be known as part of the varsity football team. Young girls fantasize over the status they will enjoy when the gang at school knows whom they are dating. We all tend to play one-upmanship with each other, and at the same time claim to be followers of Jesus who "made himself of no reputation." (Phil. 2:7 KJV)[5]

Far from being immune to such flawed assessments, we Christians too often simply put a Christian face on the idol of success. Pastor and author Jim Kallam points out:

> Scan ads in Christian periodicals and you'll reach this conclusion: Success can be yours. If you need to know how to market your church, try this or that program. . . . Listen to how we describe churches.

Our words ooze success: "Fastest growing church in the Southwest." "Largest in their denomination." "The church with the key to reaching the next generation."[6]

Kallam goes on to mention a book that identifies the top one hundred churches in America. Think about that: the top one hundred churches in America. Do you doubt size, prestige, and fame were among the criteria for making the list?

All this springs from a false assessment of success. Jesus, on the other hand, spoke a different language, a language James and John were still learning. He talked about seeking out *last* place (see Mark 9:35). He talked about taking the *lowest* position in a social setting (see Luke 14:10). He talked about including the *least* "important" people in your plans (see Luke 14:13).

Jesus' assessment of success is not preoccupied with status, power, position, and recognition. Success in God's eyes is just the opposite: a preoccupation with being last, lowest, and least.

A Flawed Agenda for Success

A flawed assessment of success was not James's and John's only problem; their actions and words also reveal a false agenda for the success they sought. But Jesus saw right through their agenda. "Jesus said to them, . . . To sit at My right or left is not Mine to give; instead, it is for those it has been prepared for" (Mark 10:39–40). He went on:

> Jesus called [his disciples] over and said to them, "You know that those who are regarded as rulers of the Gentiles dominate them, and their men of high positions exercise power over them. But it must not be like that among you. On the contrary, whoever wants to become great among you must be your servant, and whoever wants to be first among you must be a slave to all. For even the Son of Man did not come to be served, but to serve, and to give His life—a ransom for many."
> (Mark 10:42–45)

Jesus perceived that James and John were seeking advancement for the power it would give them over others. Their request to "sit at Your right and at Your left in Your glory" was a synonym for being second in authority only to Jesus and thus becoming able to "lord it over" (Mark 10:42 NKJV) everyone around them.

That's a thoroughly flawed agenda for success. But it's the agenda we share with James and John when we seek to paint ourselves with the patina of success. Campolo writes:

> When I evaluate my own attitudes, I find that the only time I am seriously tempted to lie is when it will enhance my personal status. I have a tendency to make myself out as more than I really am, to paint myself bigger than life. I exaggerate my successes, minimize my failures, and offer myself to the world as somebody who has done great things. Oh, what a sorry contrast I make to Jesus who was willing to make Himself nothing for our sakes![7]

Like James and John, we seek success because then we can "throw [our] weight around" (Mark 10:42 *The Message*). We seek success so we can feel superior to other people. We seek success so we can feel better about ourselves. But in doing so, we worship an idol because we cannot seek those things and God's kingdom at the same time:

> Sitting down, [Jesus] called the Twelve and said to them, "If anyone wants to be first, he must be last of all and servant of all." Then He took a child, had him stand among them, and taking him in His arms, He said to them, "Whoever welcomes one little child such as this in My name welcomes Me." (Mark 9:35–37)

Jesus told his followers that the key to success is servanthood *because the only godly reason to achieve success is servanthood!* Seeking success for any other reason is flirting with idolatry; it's exalting a worldly ideal above the word of Jesus. It is choosing the world's way over God's way. It is believing more in the blessings success will bring than in the blessings God gives.

I have a friend who planted a hugely "successful" church in the 1970s, a church that has since grown to host thousands of worshippers every weekend. It can be a real ego booster to preach in four services every weekend, to a thousand people at a time. But this pastor would slip out the back door of the church between services every Sunday and go to nearby businesses to offer to clean their toilets as a way of "showing God's love in a practical way."

I read about one "successful" pastor on America's West Coast who has a policy of hiring every new pastoral staff member into a temporary position: church custodian. He's interested in staffing his church with men and women who reflect Jesus' agenda for success, and so he insists that every new pastor demonstrate servanthood by cleaning the church before leading the church.

I heard about a "successful" author who wrote a best-selling book that surprised everyone, including him, by selling millions of copies and making him millions of dollars. Raised by his runaway success to a level of financial independence he had never expected, he soon set sail to serve AIDS orphans in Africa.

When our agenda in seeking success is other than service to God and others, we are embracing a flawed agenda. The key to success is servanthood because the only godly reason to achieve success is servanthood.

A Faulty Application of Success

You'd think they would learn.

Jesus had told his closest followers, "If anyone wants to be first, he must be last of all and the servant of all" (Mark 9:35). He had made clear to them that the key to success is servanthood.

He told a parable about a wedding banquet, instructing them to seek the lowest seats instead of scrambling after the most important places (see Luke 14:7–14).

Then James and John approached him and asked him to grant them seats of honor in the coming kingdom, and Jesus told them, again, "Whoever wants to be great among you must be your servant" (Mark 10:43).

You'd think they would learn.

Yet, after all that, after three years of walking with Jesus and learning from him, they still didn't get it. Luke records the disciples' excited question after Jesus' death and resurrection, when he had led them to the top of the Mount of Olives, from which they could see the Holy City of Jerusalem spread below them in all its splendor. "They asked Him, 'Lord, at this time are You restoring the kingdom to Israel?'" (Acts 1:6).

In other words, "Is our ship about to come in?" "Are you finally gonna put the Romans in their place and make us your cabinet?" "Is payday finally here?" After all that time, they still didn't get it (to be fair, they didn't yet have the Holy Spirit, who would help them put the pieces together [John 16:13]). They were still seeking worldly power because they were anticipating a faulty application of success.

Jesus corrected their misconception when he said:

> "It is not for you to know times or periods that the
> Father has set by His own authority. But you will receive
> power." (Acts 1:7–8)

Jesus' words to his closest friends reveal that he saw right through their question to the central issue, their primary concern. They were seeking success, a worldly success characterized by power and prestige. Jesus said to them, in effect, "You *will* receive power, but it will not be for the purpose you imagine." Look at the rest of his words:

> "You will receive power when the Holy Spirit has come
> upon you, and you will be My witnesses in Jerusalem, in
> all Judea and Samaria, and to the ends of the earth."
> (Acts 1:8)

That is the godly application of success. When our success results merely in our honor, we are not truly successful, not in God's eyes. When our success enhances our personal status, makes us out as more than we really are, paints us bigger than life, and presents us to the world as somebody who has done great things, then we are flirting with an idol.

But if our success brings praise to God and unequivocally communicates to the world that "[He] has done great things" (Luke 1:49), then it may rightly be called godly success because the only godly application of success is witness.

The Subtle Idolatry of Success

The idol of success is among the most subtle forms of idolatry because we are surrounded with its demands. It is also among the most intractable because its demands are incessant.

But it is not impossible to conquer. Like all forms of idolatry, its overthrow begins with repentance. It must begin with firmly and repeatedly saying "no," as Richard Foster recommends,[8] to the voices of worldly success, voices that say, "It's OK to be greedy. . . . It's OK to look out for Number One. . . . It's OK to be Machiavellian. . . . And it's *always* OK to be rich."[9] We must say "no" to the pressure to impress others with our purchases or position. We must say "no" to the tendency to seek the first place in line or in traffic. We must say "no" to the temptation to define ourselves by what others think of us.

It is impossible to do those things in our own strength, of course, which is why we must also resolutely and repeatedly say "yes" to God. We must say "yes" to *his* assessment, *his* agenda, and *his* application of success. We must agree with him that the way to be truly successful is to seek the last, lowest, and least place of all. We must agree with him that the key to success is servanthood and that the only godly application of success is witnessing to God's glory and goodness.

If you can do those things, then let me suggest three other steps to take, a three-part spiritual exercise that may help to topple the idol of success in your heart and life.

Surrender, Servanthood, and Secrecy and Silence

First, surrender your success to God. Whether you work in the home or outside the home, in the church or in the marketplace, let me strongly suggest that you physically signify your surrender by building an "altar" in your workplace. Your altar might consist of a pile of pebbles or a trophy base, a block of wood or even a picture frame. Place it where you will see it daily, even constantly (this can be in a corner of the room, a tabletop, a bookshelf, etc.). Then take a symbol of your job, career, or vocation, and place that symbol on (or in front of) the altar, asking God to help you keep it there, seeking not success in the world's eyes but using that job to bring glory to God.

Second, seek out a servant task to perform. Remember that when Jesus gathered with his twelve men in the upper room for his last Passover, he took upon himself the menial task of washing their feet (a task usually reserved for the lowest servant in the household). Or consider a pastor I know who was part of a team that was helping a widow move; he walked several times past the most disgusting kitty litter box he'd ever seen (and smelled) before realizing that he should take on that loathsome task himself (only learning later that it had been an example to someone else). So find some way each day to perform a lowly servant task. You might clean a toilet for someone, like my church planter friend does. You might volunteer to do something at church. You might help a neighbor. You might do the one thing everyone in your family hates most to do.

Finally, pursue secrecy and silence in your servanthood. In other words, look for ways to serve anonymously, unnoticed, and unheralded. Richard Foster points out that there is a risk of servanthood degenerating into "spiritual stardom," a form of service that says, "Look at how wonderful I am! Look at how much good I am accomplishing."[10] Such service would, of course, promote the same idolatry these exercises are intended to counter. So, to prevent that from happening, look for opportunities to practice secret, silent servanthood, reminding yourself that the purpose is not to be recognized as a "successful" servant but to topple the idol of success and instead exalt God to his proper place in your heart, mind, and life.

> *Heavenly Father, I do not want to pursue or reflect the world's idea of success. I do not want to install the idol of success in my beliefs and behaviors instead of you or ahead of you.*
>
> *Please cure me of a false assessment of success; save me from pursuing status, power, position, or recognition. Deliver me from the "relentless drive to enhance [my image] in the eyes of admirers."*
>
> *Heal me from having a flawed agenda for pursuing success; help me to seek not to lord it over anyone but to be like the Son of Man who "did not come to be served, but to serve, and to give His life—a ransom for many" (Mark 10:42–45). Help me to feel your pleasure in truly serving others, in literally or figuratively washing their feet, and in stooping low so that I may identify with my Lord who stooped all the way from heaven to earth for my sake.*
>
> *And please grant that my life may reflect the only godly application of success in bringing glory to you and honor to your name. Save me, too, from being proud of my humility when I spurn the pleasure of achievement and scorn compliments and praise.[11]*
>
> *Shatter the idol of success in me and be exalted to your rightful place in my heart, mind, and life, my King and my God, in Jesus' name, amen.*

TEN

The Eros Ethos

The title was provocative. The characters were pretty women. The year was 1998.

America was first exposed to the HBO television series *Sex and the City* in June of that year. In the first episode Carrie, Samantha, and Miranda made a pact at Miranda's thirty-something birthday party: to start having sex like men—that is, with no emotional attachment and no expectations other than a good time. Only one of the four women in their group, Charlotte, thought this pursuit of casual, meaningless sex might be a bad idea.

Carrie (played by Sarah Jessica Parker) strikes first, having sex with an old flame who has no objection to being used for meaningless sex. Miranda (Cynthia Nixon) warms up to Skipper, a friend of Carrie's. When Charlotte (Kristin Davis) refuses to sleep with a man on the first date, Samantha (Kim Cattrall) snags him for a one-night stand.

Carrie, left alone at the end of the evening, has trouble hailing a cab and resigns herself to walking home alone when yet another man from the party pulls to the curb and offers her a ride. She goes home with him.

This "hit" cable television show (now in syndication) enjoyed a run of six seasons. True to its title, it was about sex. And very little else.

Sex and the City is not an aberration, however. Most episodes of the successful network show *Friends* dealt with sexual subject matter. Not to mention *Will and Grace, The OC, Desperate Housewives,* and many more.

The Kaiser Foundation conducts research regarding sex on television. In a recent study of 1,114 randomly selected programs, the study discovered sexual content on 68 percent of all shows, up sharply from 56 percent just two years earlier. Not only that, but the closer you look, the worse it gets. For instance, 84 percent of all sitcoms and 89 percent of TV movies involved sex or sexually oriented language. During prime time hours, 75 percent of all shows (three in four) featured sexual content of some kind. And the participants are getting younger: in the two years between the studies, the portion of the characters having sex who were teenagers tripled.[1]

Saturated with Sex

It's not just television, of course. American culture and media are saturated with sex. From stage plays to movies, live concerts to MTV videos, sex and sexuality are everywhere. As Irving Kristol puts it, we have "soft porn in our Hollywood movies, hard porn in our cable movies and violent porn in our 'rap' music."[2] Magazines and newspapers alike use sex as a selling tool not only in advertisements but in cover art and article illustrations. An interstate drive through American cities will almost unavoidably feature frequent billboards for adult bookstores and euphemistically named "gentlemen's clubs." Many hotels offer pay-per-view porn as a part of their service.

And that barely scratches the surface, as Jerome Weeks writes in the *Dallas Morning News*:

> Porn has long been a multibillion-dollar industry—in its Internet and direct-to-DVD ghetto. But rarely has "aboveground" publishing been so saturated with sex. As Regan Books' Judith Regan put it on a recent "60 Minutes": It's the "porno-ization of the culture."
>
> In "Smut: A Sex Industry Insider (and Concerned Father) Says Enough is Enough" . . . author Guy Reavill argues there's a difference between today's sex culture and the heyday of porno chic when he began writing for publications such as Penthouse. In the 70s, he notes, as talked-about as such explicit material was, we still had to look for it. Now it seems we can barely escape it.[3]

Sex—via sexual images and content—is everywhere in our society. Sex is more prevalent in America than images of Mao Tse Tung once were in Communist China. Because, like Mao, sex has become an object of worship to us. Author Philip Yancey has written:

> When a society loses faith in God, lesser powers arise to take God's place. "Every man who knocks on the door of a brothel is looking for God," said G. K. Chesterton. In modern Europe and the U.S., sex has a near-sacred quality of mythic, numinous power. We select our sexiest individuals and accord them the status of gods and goddesses, fawning over the details of their lives, broadcasting their bodily statistics, surrounding them with *paparazzi,* rewarding them with money and status. Sex no longer points to something beyond; it becomes the thing itself, the substitute sacred.[4]

Sex is a modern substitute for the sacred and a prominently American idol. It not only distracts and detracts from the worship of the true God; it is a potent barrier to spiritual growth and blessing for many who are prone to its allure.

It is not just men who struggle with the idol of sex; women, even Christian women, often believe the *Sex and the City* variety of lies about sex and intimacy. Nor is it just the user of Internet porn or the subscriber to porn magazines who falls prey to this form of idolatry (though 33 percent of clergy and 36 percent of lay Christians admit to having visited sexually explicit Web sites).[5] It is also the vacationer at the beach or family resort, the worker on the college campus, the patron at the restaurant or sports event. Because of the sexuality that permeates our culture, many more of us are prone to sexual idolatry than we may suspect.

Stephen Arterburn and Fred Stoeker, in their book *Every Man's Battle*, say:

> You're still teaching Sunday school, still singing in the choir, still supporting your family. . . . You're getting ahead, living in a nice home with nice cars and nice clothes and a nice future. *People look to me as an example*, you say. *I'm OK.*
>
> Yet privately your conscience dims until you can't quite tell what's right or wrong anymore, watching things like *Forrest Gump* without even noticing the sexuality. . . . And nagging you is the worship. The prayer times. The distance, always the distance from God.[6]

The distance is a result not only of disobedience but also of idolatry. The worship of another god will always drive a wedge between us and the Lover of our souls—not because he will turn away but because we already have.

When Sex Is Sacred

Before we discuss the idol of sex in American culture (and in the church), we must first make clear that sex is not always idolatrous. Like other topics in this book (success, beauty, experience, etc.), sex is not intrinsically idolatrous. On the contrary, Richard Foster, in his marvelous book *Money, Sex and Power*, points out that God in his wisdom devoted an entire book of the Bible to a poetic depiction of sex as a sacred, beautiful privilege between a husband and wife. "There," Foster writes, "is sensuality without licentiousness, passion without promiscuity, love without lust."[7] He goes on to point out four important things the Bible's Song of Solomon portrays about sex:

1. Its intensity. Foster is far from the first to note the passionate, enthusiastic language of the lovers' song. When sex is sacred, it is intense—the most intense sensual experience, perhaps. "The singer goes to great lengths, piling superlative upon superlative, to show the extravagance of their love."[8] The lovers in the poem sing passionately of their joy in each other and pursue each other boldly, shamelessly. This, Foster says, is "eros without shame."[9]

2. Its restraint. "There is no crude orgy here," Foster continues, "no pawing and pounding[, no] leering and lusting."[10] It is a love that saves itself, a love that waits, a love that refuses to be "awakened" before its time (Song of Songs 3:5; 5:8; 8:4):

> No passage illustrates this better than the wedding scene. The man describes his bride-to-be as "a garden locked, a fountain sealed" (4:12). She has said no to capricious sex; she has kept her garden locked. But then we come to the wedding night, when the woman calls out, "Awake, O north wind, and come, O south wind! Blow upon my garden, let its fragrance be wafted abroad. Let my beloved come to his garden, and eat its choicest fruits" (4:16). Love's intensity. Love's restraint.[11]

3. Its mutuality. "Nowhere in this book do you find the dull story of man acting and the woman being acted upon—quite the contrary! Both are intensely involved; both initiate; both receive."[12] Foster rightly points out that even the structure of the poem itself reinforces the mutuality of the singers' love: "The man speaks, the woman speaks, the chorus sings the refrain."[13]

4. Its permanence. The depiction of sex in the Song of Solomon is about as far as it can get from Carrie, Samantha, and Miranda of *Sex and the City.*

Set me as a seal on your heart,
as a seal on your arm.
For love is as strong as death;
ardent love is as unrelenting as Sheol.
Love's flames are fiery flames,
the fiercest of all.
Mighty waters cannot extinguish love,
rivers cannot sweep it away.
If a man were to give all his wealth for love,
it would be utterly scorned. (Song of Songs 8:6–7)

The Bible leaves us in no doubt that sex does not have to be an idol. When sex is enjoyed within the intensity, restraint, mutuality, and permanence of the marriage covenant, it becomes not only healthy and wholesome but godly.

Portrait of a Sex Worshipper

The man or woman looking for insight into our modern idol of sex and sexuality can profit from a look at an ancient example: Samson, the strong man with a weakness for women. Samson's story, which is found in Judges 13–16, may provide us with a metaphor for the man or woman who is turning more and more to sex as an idol.

Judges 13 relates the circumstances of Samson's birth. He was born into a solid Israelite family. His mother, who had been unable to conceive children, learned from an angel that she would be given a son, who was to be dedicated to God as a Nazirite. Samson's parents sought direction from God in prayer, received another angelic visitation, and kept their promises to raise the boy as one who was specially devoted to God. We may trace a few parallels in Samson's story to those of us who, whether early or late in our lives, have dedicated ourselves to God and committed to following him wholeheartedly. But, like Samson, we may be "led to dumb idols—being led astray" (1 Cor. 12:2).

In God's wisdom and love, however, it may just be that the story of Samson can help us identify, recognize, and resist the characteristics of unsacred sexuality, an idol that can take us captive and not only weaken us but destroy us.

It Is Impersonal

The person who has heard the story of Samson may be surprised to notice that the Bible's introduction of him, after the account of his birth, is not an account of his strength but a depiction of his weakness. The first scene in which Samson appears in the Bible is not a scene of muscle or might but one of stubborn, impersonal sexual attraction:

> Samson went down to Timnah and saw a young
> Philistine woman there. He went back and told his
> father and his mother: "I have seen a young Philistine
> woman in Timnah. Now get her for me as a wife."
> But his father and mother said to him, "Can't you
> find a young woman among your relatives or among any
> of our people? Must you go to the uncircumcised
> Philistines for a wife?"
> But Samson told his father, "Get her for me,
> because I want her." (Judg. 14:1–3)

The Bible doesn't say that Samson "met" this Philistine woman; it says he "saw" her. He apparently didn't know this woman at all. The account, which goes on for over six hundred words, never even refers to her by name! I think that's significant.

When sex is sacred, it is intensely intimate; when it is idolatrous, it is impersonal. The woman's name apparently wasn't important to Samson. Her family apparently wasn't important to him. Her background, her values, and her religion seemed likewise unimportant. He knew only one thing: "I want her." Sexual idolatry is exactly the kind of sex that Carrie, Miranda, and Samantha pursued in the first episode of *Sex and the City*.

Arterburn and Stoeker write:

> [Idolatrous] sex is "mere sex," sex for its own sake, sex
> divorced from human relationship and contact. This is
> most clear regarding sex fantasy, pornography, and

masturbation. But even regarding sex involving a partner, the partner isn't really a "person" but a cipher,
an interchangeable part in an impersonal—almost
mechanical—process. The most intimately personal of
human behaviors becomes utterly impersonal.[14]

This is true not only of those who engage in premarital or
extramarital sex, nor only of men who attend "gentlemen's clubs"
or women who fantasize about a "hunk" in a favorite soap opera.
It is also prevalent in more subtle forms of our idolatry, such as
the sexy women on billboards or muscled men on subway ads that
engage our attention. As Richard Foster says:

Lust . . . denies relationship. Lust turns the other person
into an object, a thing, a nonperson.[15]

Is it even possible for sex between a husband and wife to be
idolatrous? Certainly, for sex fails to fulfill its sacred function any
time it is impersonal instead of intimate.

It Is Incessant

The most famous episode in Samson's life, of course, is his
fateful dalliance with Delilah. That intriguing story may teach us
many things. It may reveal that God can use the most flawed
people to accomplish his purposes. It may also depict the perils of
sin in general and sexual sin in particular. And it certainly illustrates the wisdom of the biblical admonition, "Though the lips
of the forbidden woman drip honey and her words are smoother
than oil, in the end she's as bitter as wormwood and as sharp as
a double-edged sword" (Prov. 5:3–4).

In addition to these things, the story of Samson and Delilah
may also map for us the characteristics of sexual idolatry, among
them the fact that it is incessant. The account begins:

Some time later, [Samson] fell in love with a woman
named Delilah, who lived in the Sorek Valley. The
Philistine leaders went to her and said, "Persuade him to
tell you where his great strength comes from, so we can

overpower him, tie him up, and make him helpless. Each
of us will then give you 1,100 pieces of silver."

So Delilah said to Samson, "Please tell me, where
does your great strength come from? How could someone tie you up and make you helpless?"

Samson told her, "If they tie me up with seven fresh
bowstrings that have not been dried, I will become weak
and be like any other man."

The Philistine leaders brought her seven fresh bowstrings that had not been dried, and she tied him up
with them. While the men in ambush were waiting in
her room, she called out to him, "Samson, the
Philistines are here!" But he snapped the bowstrings as a
strand of yarn snaps when it touches fire. The secret of
his strength remained unknown. (Judg. 16:4–9)

Samson apparently was not a student of the "Fool me once,
shame on you; fool me twice, shame on me" school. When
Delilah cooed and cajoled again, he gave her another story:

Then Delilah said to Samson, "You have mocked me
and told me lies! Won't you please tell me how you can
be tied up?"

He told her, "If they tie me up with new ropes that
have never been used, I will become weak and be like
any other man."

Delilah took new ropes, tied him up with them,
and shouted, "Samson, the Philistines are here!" But
while the men in ambush were waiting in her room,
he snapped the ropes off his arms like a thread.
(Judg. 16:10–12)

Clearly Samson sees through her deception, right? He has lied
to her twice to test her, right? He knows now that she can never
be trusted, right?

Then Delilah said to Samson, "You have mocked me all
along and told me lies! Tell me how you can be tied up."

He told her, "If you weave the seven braids on my
head with the web of a loom and fasten them with a pin

into the wall, I will become weak and be like any
other man."
       And while he was sleeping, Delilah wove the seven
braids on his head into the loom. She fastened the
braids with a pin and called to him, "Samson, the
Philistines are here!" He awoke from his sleep and
pulled out the pin, with the loom and the web.
(Judg. 16:13–14)

This woman is a real piece of work. Any intelligent man
would see through her pouting and persuading. No one would be
foolish enough to give in to her after being betrayed three times.
Right? Wrong:

       "How can you say, 'I love you,'" she told him,
"when your heart is not with me? This is the third time
you have mocked me and not told me what makes your
strength so great!"
       *Because she nagged him day after day and pled with
him until she wore him out,* he told her the whole truth
and said to her, "My hair has never been cut, because
I am a Nazarite to God from birth. If I am shaved, my
strength will leave me, and I will become weak and be
like any other man." (Judg. 16:15–17, author emphasis)

Samson's doom was sealed because the temptress's appeal
was incessant. We might be shocked that he would not learn
from her repeated betrayals, but for that reason the story makes
such a good metaphor for sexual idolatry. Samson did not
become smarter with every temptation; instead, his will was
weakened because the temptation never let up.
       So it is with us and the sexual images and references that
just never let up: billboards, television programs, movies, music,
e-mails, Web sites, advertisements, commercials, magazines,
catalogs, radio, books, store displays, and on and on. One of
the great dangers of this modern American idol is that it is
incessant.

It Is Idealized

One of the advantages of frequent and repeated Bible reading is the ability to read with a practiced eye. Often after repeated readings, new details and insights seem to leap off the page at the reader. Frequently those details are not the things the writer included but the glaring absences or omissions from the story. It is no different in this account of Samson and Delilah.

Notice the following verses, and then ask yourself what's missing:

> Then Delilah said to Samson, "You have mocked me and told me lies! Won't you please tell me how you can be tied up?" (Judg. 16:10)

> Then Delilah said to Samson, "You have mocked me all along and told me lies! Tell me how you can be tied up." (Judg. 16:13)

> "How can you say, 'I love you,'" she told him, "when your heart is not with me? This is the third time you have mocked me and not told me what makes your strength so great!" (Judg. 16:15)

What's missing? Apparently, Samson never—not once—pointed out the obvious to Delilah: conveniently, every time he confided in her, the Philistines showed up on his doorstep. Not once did he respond, "Why is it that when I tell you what will make me weak, I am wearing that very thing when I awake the next day?" Not once did he challenge or question her suspicious behavior.

That, too, can be taken as a metaphor for sexual idolatry. Samson apparently couldn't see Delilah's flaws. He apparently viewed her as ideally after three betrayals as he did when he first fell in love with her. He was apparently living in a dream world.

Sexual idolatry is a denial of the real in favor of a fantasy. It is like chasing after the wind. Movie sex is usually scintillating and devoid of consequences. Magazine images are airbrushed and free of blemishes. Mental fantasies end predictably and without life-shattering complications. Steve Gallagher, founder of Pure Life Ministries, puts it like this in his book *At the Altar of Sexual Idolatry*:

> In the world of sexual fantasy everything is always as he imagines it. The girl (or man) in the fantasy is extremely attractive. She acts exactly as he wants, and her only wish is to satisfy his every desire. The girl's features can be changed in an instant. One moment she is a tall blond. A few minutes later she becomes an exotic Oriental. Perhaps later she is a vivacious black girl. The variations are as numerous as the world's female population itself. Not only can the partner be changed instantly, so too, can the scenario. It may be the girl that he saw at the store that day "coming on to him." Later, it is his own personal harem. Again, the possibilities are endless.
>
> In a man's world of imagination, everything is perfect. He does not have to deal with rejection. These dream girls all love him; none refuse to be with him. He never has to deal with impotence or nervousness either; everything goes smoothly. The girl is always flawless. There are no obnoxious odors, menstrual periods, diseases, or lack of interest. She does not act rudely, and she is not critical of him. She is not looking to take advantage of him or get his money. She will be willing to perform any desired sexual act because she lives to serve him. Finally, he does not need to worry about being caught by his wife or arrested by the authorities. In his perfect little dream world, nothing ever goes wrong.[16]

Our idol is an idealized idol. It wears a glittering mask, a shiny veneer. If only we could see it truly, we would recoil in horror, in repulsion; but like Samson, we are blinded by its idealized appearance.

It Is Injurious

Samson's story does not end well. We know that from Sunday school. But we shake our heads at his foolhardiness even as we imitate it:

> When Delilah realized that [Samson] had told her the whole truth, she sent this message to the Philistine leaders: "Come one more time, for he has told me the whole truth." The Philistine leaders came to her and brought the money with them.
>
> Then she let him fall asleep on her lap and called a man to shave off the seven braids on his head. In this way, she rendered him helpless, and all his strength left him. Then she cried, "Samson, the Philistines are here!" When he awoke from his sleep, he said, "I will escape as I did before and shake myself free." But he did not know that the LORD had left him. (Judg. 16:18–20)

The Bible says the Lord had left Samson, though Samson's spiritual senses were too dull to notice. Long before sexual idolatry is exposed, it takes a heavy toll, as Steve Gallagher describes:

> The sex addict does not realize the negative effect it has on his daily life. A fresh illustration of this comes to me from a scene I witnessed the other night. . . . Two men [were stacking chairs]. One of them was about thirty and grossly overweight. The other was a physically fit young man of about twenty-two. The young man would grab a couple of chairs at a time and, in almost a sprint, energetically whisk them to where they belonged. However, the heavy-set man would pick up a chair with great effort and slowly make his way across the room with it, laboring every step of the way. Such is the case with the man [or woman] who is bogged down with the weight of sexual sin. Even the smallest tasks that most people can routinely handle become extremely burdensome to him. His poor wife cannot comprehend why her husband is unable to spend a little time with their son. She does not understand this taxing load he is

carrying around in life. All of his energy is being exhausted to maintain and to pursue his secret life. It is like a computer with eight megabytes of RAM trying to run a program which requires thirty-two megabytes. The inner strength and capability is simply not available.

Paul describes the imaginations of a man given over to sin as being "vain." They are as empty as the illusive mirages that deceive thirsty souls traveling through the desert, offering no benefit to a man's life. They are utterly worthless. In fact, they are worse. Not only are they devoid of any reality, but they also have the power to deplete a man's soul of anything that is of substance or value. The more a man gives himself over to a per-verted thought life, the more his moral character rots from the inside out, leaving a great void inside. . . . Merlin Carothers says this:

There is something intriguing and mystifying about our ability to imagine things known and unknown. To God, that ability is sacred. He does not want it misused. And that is exactly why evil forces have an intense desire to see that ability misused. Our minds are the battle-ground; our imaginations are the trophy to be won.

If we use our imaginative power to visualize any-thing that represents lust or impurity, we are in direct conflict with God's will. Men enjoy using the power of imagination to create a multitude of images that God has forbidden. For example, when a man sees a woman who is attractive to him [and uses] his imagination to [sin, he] has taken God's special, holy gift and consumed it upon the altar of lust.[17]

What Samson learned, many televangelists, pastors, Sunday school teachers, and church members have learned. Idol worship always ends in destruction. Sexual idolatry will cost you dearly. It may cost you everything.

Overcoming the Eros Ethos

The idol of sex and sexuality is one of the most stubborn idols a person can face. But, while it is stubborn, it is an idol; it is no match for the power of the true God: "We know that 'an idol is nothing in the world' and that 'there is no God but one' " (1 Cor. 8:4).

Therefore, like all false gods, sexual idolatry can be cast down through repentance and submission to God. So, in the name of Jesus, I urge you to repent of all sexual idolatry:

- Repent of entertaining secret, impure thoughts.
- Repent of staring at sexy strangers.
- Repent of lingering looks at alluring advertisements.
- Repent of using pornography.
- Repent of treating sex as a substitute for intimacy, instead of enjoying it as a means of intimacy with your spouse.
- Repent of seeking out sexually arousing articles, books, magazines, catalogs, or Web sites.
- Repent of enjoying sex scenes in movies.
- Repent of selecting movies, television shows, sporting events, and eating establishments for the promise of titillation.
- Repent of creating fantasies about a friend or acquaintance.
- Repent of voyeurism (secretly watching people or things that stimulate you sexually).
- Repent of treating your spouse as an object.
- Repent of making sexual remarks or telling dirty jokes.

If even a single one of those lines above describes a recurring practice of yours, stop reading now, and take time to pour out your confession—in as much detail as you can summon—to God, turning your heart and will away from those practices, and thanking him for his forgiveness in Christ.

Having done that, the level of your awareness and involvement will dictate where you must go next. Arterburn and Stoeker recommend a "first line of defense" of reminding yourself as often as necessary: *this idolatry threatens everything I hold most dear.* You may want to repeat that phrase to yourself now, several times, and repeat it every time temptation presents itself.

In addition, choose at least one of the following as a spiritual formation exercise, praying as you do that God will bless your effort and use it to deliver you from sexual idolatry:

1. Read one or more of the following books:
- *Every Man's Battle,* by Steve Arterburn and Fred Stoeker with Mike Yorkey
- *Every Woman's Battle,* by Steve Arterburn and Fred Stoeker with Mike Yorkey
- *Every Young Man's Battle* (more appropriate for single men), by Steve Arterburn and Fred Stoeker with Mike Yorkey
- *Every Young Woman's Battle* (more appropriate for single women), by Shannon Ethridge and Steve Arterburn
- *Eros Defiled,* by John White
- *At the Altar of Sexual Idolatry,* by Steve Gallagher

2. Make a covenant with your eyes (see Job 31:1). Try to go twenty-four hours without looking on anything erotic (other than your spouse, of course, if you're married). If you fail, begin again the next morning. Continue until your covenant has developed into a habit.

3. Erect boundaries that will honor your covenant. For example, if sexual idolatry has prompted you to purchase pornography in the past, steer clear of stores that will put temptation in your path. If Internet porn has been a problem, purchase filtering software and give someone else the password (or use accountability software, such as that provided free by www.xxxchurch.com). If you're tempted by a past relationship, take whatever measures are necessary to avoid that temptation in the future, even to the point of asking for a transfer or moving to a different town (see Matt. 5:29; 18:9).

4. Become accountable to someone about your sexual thought life and behavior, allowing that person (or group) to encourage you toward greater faithfulness.

Father, I believe that your divine power has given me every-thing I need for life and godliness through my knowledge of you who called me by your own glory and goodness. I also believe that you have given me your very great and precious promises, so that through them I may participate in the divine nature and escape the corruption in the world, and in my life, caused by evil desires (see 2 Pet. 1:3–4).

Please deliver me from all forms of sexual idolatry. Change my way of thinking. Change my way of acting. Change the way I respond to the incessant flow of sexual stimuli in the world around me. Help me to be more than victorious through you and your love for me. Help me to obey you and reflect you in all I do, in Jesus' name, amen.

ELEVEN

The Burger King Way

Herman was his name. Hermano, actually. He was from Venezuela, and he was the freshman college roommate of my friend Ted.

Ted once described taking Herman to an American supermarket for the first time. Ted anticipated dashing in, picking up a few items, and breezing out. But Herman stopped dead in his tracks and gazed around in awe. He strolled the aisles, absorbing the bountiful shelves and cases like a museum visitor.

"I have never seen such variety," he explained later. At home, he said, there was no lack of groceries in the store. "But here there is not just milk to buy. There is milk of all kinds and all sizes. There is not just lettuce but many kinds of lettuce. There is not just Tabasco sauce but this kind and that kind."

He shook his head, clearly amazed but also confused. "Why do Americans need ten different kinds of toilet paper?" he asked.

Have It Your Way

I don't remember what I said to Herman back then. Maybe I explained that some Americans like plush toilet paper, and others just want what's cheapest. Maybe I said that some folks prefer two-ply toilet paper and others don't care. Maybe I talked about how some people choose a certain color or design for aesthetic purposes or that some consumers are loyal to a particular brand. I don't remember.

But that's OK because it's not about toilet paper. That's what I should have said to Herman. I should have explained that Americans value choice. We consider it our right, granted to us by the Constitution. We are free to choose, free to be and do and have whatever we want.

It shows up every day, in all areas of our lives. It's how we like our hamburgers ("Have it your way"); our television ("Welcome to iCONTROL, a new service that allows you to choose from a variety of movies and programs to watch when it's convenient for you"); our radio ("America's most popular satellite radio service gives you the power to choose what you want to hear—wherever and whenever you want it"[1]); our beverages ("Would you like Coke, Diet Coke, Cherry Coke, Vanilla Coke, or C2?"); our in-flight meals ("Beef, chicken, or vegetarian?"); and our church ("We offer a contemporary service at 9:00 and traditional worship at 10:30").

This veneration of choice extends to our children: parents can choose the sex of their baby.[2] It extends to our sexual identity: an estimated one thousand Americans every year choose to change their gender via "sexual reassignment surgery."[3] It even extends to the time and circumstances of our death: in the past ten years more than two hundred people in Oregon (where assisted suicide is legal) have killed themselves with a doctor's help.[4] And, of course, it extends to the survival of our unborn children ("Protect a woman's right to choose.").

Choice in America has become something people are willing to pay for, fight for, even die for. But for many of us, this insistence on having it our way is more than a preference and far more than a privilege. Many of us value choice so highly that it becomes a religion for us. Even an idol.

Choice Itself Is Not Bad

William J. Doherty, director of the Marriage and Family Therapy Program at the University of Minnesota, believes choice has become a modern American idol. The author of the book *Take Back Your Marriage,* Doherty has said: "We worship choice and options more than anything else. . . . We've bought [into] a cultural ideology."[5]

But choice itself is not a bad thing, of course; if it were, God would not have repeatedly offered his people a choice. Way back in the beginning, God placed Adam in the lush tropical garden of Eden, saying:

> "You are free to eat from any tree of the garden, but
> you must not eat from the tree of the knowledge of
> good and evil, for on the day you eat from it, you will
> certainly die." (Gen. 2:16–17)

"You are free," God said, free to choose from the luxurious variety of delights God placed in the garden for man's enjoyment. "But you must not," God said. One of your choices would be evil and bring about dire consequences. If choice itself were a bad thing, God would not have installed choice as a feature of the first human community.

Later, after delivering his people from slavery in Egypt and guiding them through a contentious forty years in the desert, God laid down instructions to be observed once the people crossed the Jordan and were finally in the promised land. They were to gather in an antiphonal assembly on the slopes of Mt. Gerizim and Mt. Ebal in their new land and thunderously pronounce the blessings and curses that would follow the choice to follow or reject God's commands:

I call heaven and earth as witnesses against you today
that I have set before you life and death, blessing and
curse. *Choose life* so that you and your descendants may
live, love the LORD your God, obey Him, and remain
faithful to Him. For He is your life, and He will prolong
your life in the land the LORD swore to give to your
fathers Abraham, Isaac, and Jacob. (Deut. 30:19–20,
italics added)

A mere generation later, when Joshua assembled all the tribes
of Israel at Shechem to deliver his valedictory address, he said:

Therefore, fear the LORD and worship Him in sincerity
and truth. Get rid of the gods your ancestors worshiped
beyond the Euphrates River and in Egypt, and worship
the LORD. But if it doesn't please you to worship the
LORD, *choose for yourselves* today the one you will worship. . . . As for me and my family, we will worship the
LORD. (Josh. 24:14–15, italics added)

And, finally, allow me just one more example. Centuries after
Israel renewed their covenant with Yahweh before Joshua,
the nation had been led into idolatry by a king and queen who
"abandoned the LORD's commandments and followed the Baals"
(1 Kings 18:18). So God's prophet, a man named Elijah, sum-
moned the nation to gather at Mount Carmel overlooking the
Plains of Jezreel. There,

Elijah approached all the people and said, "How long
will you hesitate between two opinions? If Yahweh is
God, follow Him. But if Baal, follow him." But the
people didn't answer him a word. (1 Kings 18:21)

It took a dramatic showdown and a supernatural fireworks
display to persuade the people to make their choice that day
(1 Kings 18:39), but the point is: God's prophet showed them
clearly that the choice was theirs.

In the garden, at Mt. Ebal and Mt. Gerizim, at Shechem, and
again on Mount Carmel, God presented his people with a clear
choice: life or death, good or evil, obedience or rebellion, Yahweh

or Baal. It is not choice itself that is a bad thing; it is our exaltation of choice, our prioritization of it as a standard and a value that can become a false god in our lives.

Choice Alone Is Not Enough

Our cable or satellite-television systems may deliver two hundred viewing choices to our living rooms, but as a birthday card I received recently stated, "A universal remote control does not, in fact, allow you to control the universe."

No matter how many choices we may demand, no matter how many choices we may have, choice alone is not enough. How many times have you scanned *TV Guide* or flipped through all two hundred channels, only to complain, "There's nothing on"?

Choice is not a virtue. Choice is not necessarily even an advantage. It can be a blessing or a curse.

As Herman discovered on his first trip through an American supermarket, there is such a thing as too many choices. Choices can confuse and distract. For example, have you ever tried to order from a ten-page restaurant menu? Have you ever been sent to the grocery store to buy diapers and been stymied by the seemingly endless array of sizes and styles? Or felt overwhelmed by a car salesman's presentation of the new car options from which you have to choose?

On a much more serious note, of course, America's exaltation of choice has actually eroded our liberties. Take author and pastor Randy Alcorn, for example. Alcorn participated in a number of nonviolent abortion clinic protests, for which he was sued by the clinics. One court leveled an 8.4 million-dollar judgment against him and his group, the largest judgment against pro-lifers in history.

When Randy determined that he could not in good conscience pay a clinic that would use the money to kill children, the authorities came to his church to garnish his wages. He was forced to resign from his pastoral position. He was forced to divest himself of all income and possessions because anything he earned or owned would be paid to the clinic. Since that court ruled against him, he has refused to earn or own anything and says he will do so as long as doing so would fund abortions.

In Randy's case our cultural pursuit of sex without consequences (in which we have made the ability to kill unborn children into a "civil right") deprived him of his job, home, and possessions.[6]

Choice alone is not enough. It is not always a virtue. Choice—especially the kinds of choices our culture exalts—can be like a pet tiger; it can turn on you.

Choice Improperly Used Is Idolatry

Prior to his death Moses gathered the nation of Israel together and urged them to renew their covenant with God in the new land they were about to enter. He reminded them that God had brought about a mighty deliverance for them; "For you know," he said, "how we lived in the land of Egypt and how we came directly through the nations you passed through; and you saw their detestable things and their idols of wood, stone, silver and gold that they had with them" (Deut. 29:16–17 *Complete Jewish Bible*).

Then Moses urged them—and through them the generations that would follow (Deut. 29:14–15)—to use their freedom to make proper, godly choices instead of turning to idolatry:

> "Let there not be among you a man, woman, family or
> tribe whose heart turns away from ADONAI our God
> to go and serve the gods of those nations. Let there not
> be among you a root bearing such bitter poison and
> wormwood. If there is such a person, when he hears the
> words of this curse, he will bless himself secretly, saying
> to himself, 'I will be all right, even though I will stub-
> bornly keep doing whatever I feel like doing; so that
> I, although "dry," [sinful,] will be added to the
> "watered" [righteous].' But ADONAI our God will
> not forgive him. Rather, the anger and jealousy of

ADONAI will blaze up against that person."
(Deut. 29:18–20a *Complete Jewish Bible*)

When you and I allow ourselves to think that we can use our luxurious freedoms to "stubbornly keep doing whatever [we] feel like doing," we are rebellious. Journalist Marshall Allen writes:

> We buy into the mantras "the customer is always right,"
> and "have it your way." The result is a belief that we can
> operate autonomously. . . . This warped brand of
> American freedom can easily lead to self-worship—which
> separates us from God. It lessens our conviction to strive
> for God's will, and can even taint our efforts to share
> our faith with others.[7]

To the extent that you and I adopt a laissez-faire attitude, a "live and let live" philosophy toward right and wrong, we are worshipping the false god of choice. If we become inured to such things as obscenity, profanity, pornography, abortion, and prostitution because "people should be free to choose" such things, we are bowing to the god of choice. If we accept our culture's twisted view that "all choices are created equal"—what's right for me isn't necessarily right for you—we are exalting choice above Adonai our God.

If we delude ourselves into thinking that we are the captains of our own destinies, if we insist on choosing how we follow Jesus, if we willfully choose sin because we know God forgives, if we choose our church based on our preferences instead of a desire to please God, then we are "blessing ourselves secretly," to use Moses' phrase. To quote Marshall Allen again:

> Perhaps we have decided—although we'd never say it
> aloud to our Christian friends—that our money is our
> own. We'll give a pittance to support our church, or other
> ministries, but decline to give sacrificially and keep the
> largesse to spend as we please. Maybe we're refusing to
> speak to a friend or family member after a relatively minor
> conflict. God commands us to reconcile with one another,
> but we don't want to. In these cases, we're elevating our
> desires over God's design for our lives. Any number of

factors can contribute to these attitudes: greed, pride and materialism included. But each is also justified by a belief that we're free to operate as we please.[8]

When we are blinded by our freedom into thinking we will be all right because we're Americans, we have choices, we can do whatever we want, then we are deceived. But when we use our freedom of choice to glorify God and obey him, then we are "free indeed" (John 8:36 NIV).

Paul, the great church planter of the first century, underscores that point in a letter he wrote to the churches that were scattered throughout the province of Galatia. He had started some of those churches and had a father's love for them. So naturally he was concerned when he heard disturbing reports about the new Christ followers in these churches. He heard that they, who had found freedom from sin and the law and new life in Christ, were being persuaded to return again to their former way of life.

So he wrote the letter we call "Galatians" today. In it, he said, "Christ has liberated us into freedom" (Gal. 5:1). In other words, God has set us free. He endorses our freedom to choose. He *wants* us to choose. But choice is not a virtue; it is the *means* by which we can become virtuous.

After Paul says, "Christ has liberated us into freedom" (Gal. 5:1), he continues:

> Therefore stand firm and don't submit again to a yoke of slavery. . . . For you are called to freedom, brothers; only don't use this freedom as an opportunity for the flesh, but serve one another through love. (Gal. 5:1, 13)

God calls us to freedom, giving us a choice, not because choice itself is right (or wrong) but because giving us a choice makes it possible for us to choose to do right, to say yes to him.

Our situation is much like that of the coast-to-coast airline passenger who was asked by the flight attendant, "Would you like dinner?"

"What are my choices?" the traveler asked.

"Yes or no," came the answer.

He gives us freedom for one purpose and one purpose only: so we can choose obedience and righteousness. He gives us choices not so we can do whatever we want but so we can do the right thing. Peter, the Galilean fisherman who was one of the first to follow Jesus, put it this way: "As God's slaves, live as free people, but don't use your freedom as a way to conceal evil" (1 Pet. 2:16).

Choice that is used to seek God and follow hard after him (see Ps. 63:8 KJV) is in little or no danger of becoming idolatrous. But choice that is used to bless ourselves secretly while we stubbornly keep doing whatever we feel like doing has already crossed the line into idolatry.

Most of us, of course, probably spend most of our "free time" between those two extremes. We may not constantly—or even consistently—make godly choices, but neither do we think we're willfully using our freedom "as a way to conceal evil" (1 Pet. 2:16). But subtle idolatry is no less harmful to our lives and our walks with God than blatant idolatry; in some ways it is more so because it's more deceptive.

The Choice Is Yours

The purpose of this book is not to provoke condemnation or promote legalism. Neither is it intended to make us into navel-gazers as Christians, constantly questioning ourselves or our motives, always afraid that we're committing some idolatry, consciously or unconsciously. But it is designed as a tool that will allow the Holy Spirit of God to shine a light into a corner of your heart that you may not have examined before, or even been aware of, and reveal any idol that may be stunting your spiritual growth or preventing you from experiencing all the blessings God longs to bestow on you.

Ironically, God gives you the freedom, the choice, to examine your heart and life. He calls you to consider whether you have made a deity, large or small, of "choice" and, if so, repent and experience his forgiveness, cleansing, and restoration. As with all forms of idolatry, recognition and repentance are the crucial first steps.

If God *is* showing you ways you have esteemed and exalted this god of choice above him and his commands, then take your repentance a step further. Begin every day this week by submitting your every decision to God, and ask him to guide your choices (if it will help you, write a reminder in your calendar or on an index card you can post on your bathroom mirror or car dashboard). Then, as often as possible throughout the day, renew your prayer. At the end of each day, reflect on the decisions you made (you may even list every decision you can recall in a notebook or prayer journal) and see how many decisions you made after seeking God's guidance instead of on your own. Try each day to decrease the percentage of self-guided choices you make, increasing the percentage of choices you make under God's direction.

Finally, if you're interested in a challenge, try this: for the next twenty-four hours (or, if your job makes this exercise impractical on a weekday, a twenty-four-hour period in the near future), let *others* make as many choices for you as possible (for example, you might ask a coworker to order your lunch, wait for a kind driver to wave you into traffic, or—gasp!—allow your children to control the radio in the car). And keep this in mind: the degree to which you struggle with this exercise may indicate whether "choice" has become an idol in your heart.

> *Awesome God, what a perversion of your kindness and grace it is to exalt into an idol the freedom of choice you have granted us as human beings. How utterly ungrateful we are to take the choice you give us as men and women and use it to break your heart. How sorry I am for any tendency of my heart to use this freedom as an opportunity for the flesh (see Gal. 5:13), as a way to conceal evil (see 1 Pet. 2:16) and bless myself secretly, saying to myself, "I will be all right, even though I will stubbornly keep doing whatever I feel like doing" (Deut. 29:19 Complete Jewish Bible). Please save me from such tendencies, and help me instead to cast all idols far from my heart and life. Teach me to live in the freedom you give me, standing firm, pleasing you, and serving those around me through love, in Jesus' name, amen.*

TWELVE

The Passion for Fashion

At first it was just cable shows like The Learning Channel's *What Not to Wear* and Bravo's *Queer Eye for the Straight Guy*. But the rash quickly spread, and worsened, into shows depicting surgical makeovers: ABC launched *Extreme Makeover,* a series featuring an "Extreme Team" of the nation's top plastic surgeons, eye surgeons, and cosmetic dentists, along with a talented team of hairstylists, makeup artists, and personal trainers. Each episode depicted two ordinary people, shown first in an unflattering, ridicule-inviting "before" phase, undergoing various operations and tutorials that culminated in a climactic unveiling of the effects of their "Extreme Makeover"—always to tears, applause, and congratulations.

In today's era of television, of course, no idea, good or bad, goes unimitated. So Fox Television soon spawned *The Swan,* which turned the "extreme makeover" idea into a beauty competition. On this show women go through plastic surgery, cosmetic dentistry, and fitness training, as well as counseling and coaching sessions. After three months (during which time the cameras have been rolling, of course, though the women are never permitted a peek in the mirror), the "experts" unveil these self-admitted "ugly ducklings" they have transformed into "swans." At the end of the season, the most dramatically transformed contestants square off in the "Swan Beauty Pageant" to determine that season's grand-prize winner.

Perhaps the most extreme entry into the "makeover show" genre was MTV's series, *I Want a Famous Face*. This series depicted the transformation of twelve young people who, like the contestants on *Extreme Makeover* or *The Swan*, want a makeover, complete with plastic surgery. But these makeovers are different. Their purpose is not to correct crooked teeth or weight problems but to make each contestant look like his or her favorite celebrity idol.

Can anyone not see that things are out of control? Is there any doubt that such shows depict not mere desires but severe dysfunctions? Does anyone believe that a craving for beauty and style that creates a whole new television genre, plastic surgery for entertainment, is a healthy thing?

Such shows may be fascinating to many, but they should also disturb us. They should concern us. They should probably even shame us. And we can't just cluck our tongues, blame TV executives, and shake our heads at their shocking lack of decency and propriety. Because, in this case at least, TV is a mere reflection of our own idolatry.

Our Madness

Oh, don't worry. I'm not suggesting that watching a television show like *The Swan* makes you an idolater (though I much prefer *What Not to Wear* myself). It's not the viewing that presents the greatest danger; it's the doing.

Christians probably don't represent a large percentage of the viewing audience for most makeover shows. But many of us reflect the same attitudes that gave rise to those kinds of shows. To be fair, some of us have healthy attitudes. Some of us merely value youth, beauty, slimness, and physical fitness; but others of us go much further. Some of us worship them.

Now don't get me wrong. There's nothing wrong with youth, beauty, slimness, and physical fitness (I was young once myself). But some of us fight aging so desperately that we exalt youth into an ideal. Some of us spend so much time, effort, and money striving for beauty and slimness that anyone who's watching closely can see who our true god is. Some of us place such an emphasis on fitness that our workout rooms have become shrines.

Our drift into idolatry seldom happens suddenly or quickly. More often it is a gradual succumbing to the pressures around us, a bit-by-bit process of adopting the affections and allegiances that are prevalent in our culture. Take Solomon, for example. The early years of his reign were characterized by heartfelt prayers (1 Kings 3:6–9; 8:15–53), wise rulings (1 Kings 3:16–28), and passionate service to Yahweh (1 Kings 8–9). But later the Bible records:

> When Solomon was old, his [many] wives seduced him to follow other gods. His heart was not completely with the LORD his God, as his father David's heart had been. Solomon followed Ashtoreth, the goddess of the Sidonians, and Milcom, the detestable idol of the Ammonites. Solomon did what was evil in the LORD's sight, and unlike his father David, he did not completely follow the LORD. (1 Kings 11:4–6)

So it is with us. We don't set out to lift up these ideals of personal appearance—youth, beauty, slimness, and physical fitness—into an idol, but gradually, like Solomon, we are all too prone to adopt the gods of the people around us and those closest to us. We pay more attention to the pretty child. We color or comb our hair to look more youthful. We diet incessantly, always striving—even praying—to improve our appearance. We join a health club that we don't have time to attend, pay a tanning salon to substitute for the time we don't have to spend outdoors, and then we have to buy skin care products to prevent the tanning process from damaging our skin. How crazy is that?

Of course, you may think that, as a Christ follower, you're reasonably immune from the allure of this idol that exalts personal appearance. But be careful. Some of the worst examples of this idolatry can be found on Christian television, at Christian conferences, and in Christian bookstores, adding our so-called "Christian" version to the idolatry that pervades America's secular culture.

It should be no surprise, then, that our own kids are ill equipped to recognize and resist this form of idolatry, as journalist Marshall Allen reports:

> The shock still registered on Mark's face as he told me
> about a current challenge he was facing in his youth
> ministry. He had arrived for Bible study at the house of
> a 17-year-old girl in his youth group—the daughter of
> one of the church's top leaders—and learned she
> wouldn't be attending the meeting. She was in her bed-
> room, recovering from a recent surgery where she
> received breast implants, a gift from mommy and daddy.
> I live in L.A., where silicon breasts are practically
> all-season fashion accessories, but it's [nonetheless]
> surprising to me.[1]

Of course, we don't know all that went into that family's deci-sion, but it sure looks like this passion for fashion and beauty is out of control, even among us who follow Christ. That girl's sit-uation and those parents' decision might make a little more sense to us if we knew the circumstances, but it certainly seems extreme. In any case, wouldn't it be nice, to paraphrase the pop singer Billy Joel, to know why we go to such extremes?

Our Motivation

There's a fascinating historical account in the Old Testament that may help to shed some light on our culture's tendency to worship idealized standards of personal appearance. It happened during the ministry of the prophet Elisha. Jezebel and Ahab, queen and king of Israel, had made their nation into a spiritual wasteland. In spite of the ministry of the prophet Elijah and his successor, Elisha, Jezebel had continued her malignant influence as her sons—first Ahaziah, then Joram—became king after her husband's death. So Elisha, acting in obedience to God's command, anointed Jehu to take Joram's place as king.

Let's allow Walter Wangerin, in his masterful *The Book of God*, to pick up the story:

> Jezebel and Joram were in the queen's apartments, eating delicate roasts of African monkey and drinking the famous wines of Syria, skins from Helbon and from Uzal, both.
>
> In the midst of this meal, a watchman asked to speak with King Joram.
>
> He was admitted to the room.
>
> "My lord," he said, but his eyes kept straying toward the presence of a genuine force, Jezebel. "While I was watching from the tower by the gate, I saw a company of soldiers riding at great speed from the east. They are armed. They are not messengers."
>
> Joram said, "Send a horseman out to meet them. Ask if they come in peace."
>
> The watchman bowed and left. But within the hour he returned, anxious and perplexed.
>
> "I sent the horseman as you commanded, sir," he said. "But when he reached them, and when they had spoken together, he joined them! He drew his sword and is riding this way with them!"
>
> Jezebel said, "Send a second man. Send a captain and an equal company of horsemen. Arm them."
>
> "I will," the watchman said. He hurried from the room.
>
> Neither the queen nor the king ate now. Jezebel had risen to her feet and was striding about the room. "From the east," she said. "There is no close enemy in the east. Except—"

The watchman burst in without asking leave.

"Madam! Sir! The captain and his company have joined the warriors, too! They're coming with a hard determination. They are walking their mounts!"

Jezebel said, "Can you identify these people? Do you know their tribe or race?"

The watchman lowered his eyes. "Yes," he said.

"Then who are they?" Jezebel's eyes flashed. Her beauty was a deadly thing.

"Israelites," said the watchman.

"What? Our own forces?" The queen snapped erect. "Answer me, watchman: could you tell who leads them?"

The watchman whispered, "Jehu, the son of Nimshi, commander of your armies."

Jezebel spoke in a low, honeyed voice: "Joram, go out yourself. He is your subordinate."

The king was not dressed for combat. But he went, and Jezebel went out of the palace after him. When Joram rode out of the city gates, she mounted the wall and watched him go, a bodyguard of three.

When the coming company saw King Joram approach from the city, the men halted in a semicircle, Jehu in front of all.

Joram cried, "Jehu! Jehu, son of Nimshi, is it peace?"

The grim commander said, "What peace, when the whores of Jezebel fill the land?"

He had not yelled the words, but Jezebel heard them. It was the very language of that wilderness lizard, Elijah.

The scene in the distance took on a dream-like quality. Everything moved slowly, now, detached from Jezebel's immediate attention—though she felt she knew exactly what was going to happen.

Jehu the Israelite drew an arrow from his quiver. Joram her son wheeled his mount around and whipped it toward Samaria, crying, "Treachery! Treachery!"

Jehu took a thousand years to draw the arrow taut in his bow, and the arrow sailed in a beautiful arc, like a rainbow. It sank into her son's back between the shoulder blades. He spread his arms and soared from his horse, higher and higher. Jezebel closed her eyes, and the whole scene vanished.

She returned to her palace and ascended to her apartments above the central entrance.

In a private room Jezebel sat down at a table where ointments and powders were arranged, and she began to groom herself. She anointed her flesh with oil. She coiled her long hair on her head in oriental fashion. She drew black lines of antimony along the edges of her eyelids, so that the whites became a blaze of beauty. She covered herself in purple raiment and gold embroidery at the bosom, and then she walked to the window and threw open the lattice and stood there, while Jehu, the commander of the armies of her son, rode into Samaria.

Jezebel stood like a cedar tree, majestic and immovable. She said, "Is it peace?"

Jehu leaped to the ground, looking around for the source of the question. It had fallen upon him from on high.

"Is it peace?" Jezebel repeated, and Jehu saw her. So she made her voice a thick run of honey: "Do you come to my city in peace, you murderer of your master?"

Jehu did not answer her. . . . [but] opened his mouth and bellowed, "Who is on my side?"

Jezebel felt the presence of four servants in her chambers, eunuchs. She smelled them. They wore a delicate calamus. "Who is on my side?" Jehu bellowed, and the eunuchs stepped up behind the queen of Israel, two on her left, two on her right.

"Throw the woman down to the dogs!" the man commanded. She felt the soft hands of her servants. They lifted her bodily, tilted her from the window, and dropped her. She fell without a sound, turning once in the air and striking her skull on the pavement below, where she died.[2]

It's quite a story (found in the Bible in 2 Kings 9). But one small detail is utterly striking. When the cagey queen saw that "the jig was up," so to speak, with her son killed and the commander of his armies turning his horse toward her palace, she went to her boudoir and dolled herself up. What was that about? Some people think she hoped to seduce Jehu (I recall a favorite seminary professor of mine who, at this point in his Old Testament survey class, would draw his handkerchief from his pocket and wave it, affecting a female voice to imitate Jezebel, calling, "Yoohoo, Jehu!"). But I don't think that's what was happening that day in Samaria.

I agree with C. F. Keil, the Old Testament scholar, who suggests that Jezebel did this "that she might present an imposing appearance to Jehu and die as a queen."[3] Either way, I believe her intention is revealing because it says something about why we "go to extremes" in our pursuit of youth, beauty, slimness, and fitness.

Can you imagine knowing that your final moments of life are upon you and using them to apply makeup and do your hair? That's what Jezebel did, and there seems to be only one reason for her to do such a thing: a stubborn intention to leave life as impressively as possible. She saw the end approaching and resolved that she would face it as she had lived: stunningly, arrogantly, impressively, richly. If she couldn't preserve her position as a powerful queen, she would at least present a queenly corpse.

It is no less true with us. Our attention and allegiance to personal appearance serves one purpose and only one purpose. That is, to impress other human beings. Our motivation is to please men, not God. We know that "man looks at the outward appearance, but the LORD looks at the heart" (1 Sam. 16:7 NIV), so we know we are not primarily striving for God's approval when we give undue or excessive attention to our appearance. There may be any number of other factors that contribute to our efforts: we may be trying to flirt, we may be dressing to impress, or we may just be looking for that boost in spirit when someone mistakes us for our daughter's sister. But in so doing we are not pursuing God but something else. And in that pursuit is the root of idolatry.

Our Medicine

No one in his or her right mind wants to be (or look) old, ugly, obese, and out of shape. But those are not God's standards for us who follow Christ any more than he wants us to exalt youth, beauty, slimness, and fitness to the place of a god in our lives.

The solution for unhealthy attitudes toward our physical appearance is not *other* unhealthy attitudes but healthy attitudes, godly ones. And those kinds of attitudes are exactly what God's Word prescribes for us.

In a letter to his pastoral protégé, Paul, the great church planter of the first century, wrote to Timothy:

> I . . . want women to dress modestly, with decency
> and propriety, not with braided hair or gold or pearls
> or expensive clothes, but with good deeds, appropriate
> for women who profess to worship God.
> (1 Tim. 2:9–10 NIV)

I think it's important to note first that, while these verses are addressed specifically to women, we need not apply them only to women. After all, the preceding verse in that passage admonishes "men everywhere to lift up holy hands in prayer, without anger or disputing" (1 Tim. 2:8 NIV). Should we infer that it would not be Paul's wish or God's will for women everywhere to do the same? Or is it far more likely that Paul was instructing Timothy, his pastoral protégé, in ways that were specific to the condition and culture in which Timothy ministered?

I'm convinced that the principles Paul shared with Timothy are timeless and universal, appropriate for both men and women, while his immediate application was to the customs (like braided hair and expensive jewelry and clothes) that had been spreading among women in the new Christian communities in which

Timothy ministered. Paul identified four principles that outline a godly approach to youth, beauty, slimness, and fitness.

Modesty

Paul's prescription to Timothy was for "women to dress modestly" (1 Tim. 2:9 NIV), rather than pridefully and expensively. He may not have had Jezebel in mind when he wrote (or dictated) those words, but they certainly contrast with Jezebel's example. Ahab's wicked queen planned to show everyone, including her son's killer and usurper, that she was and always would be a queen. She intended to die as proudly as she had lived.

And so it is sometimes with us. Behind our passion for fashion is a certain pride, a desire to elevate ourselves above those around us, a need to set ourselves apart. We know that when we wear that ensemble, heads will turn, people will take notice, and we will enjoy their admiration.

But God's will for you and me, of course, is for us to find what we need in him. He longs for us to feel his approval to such an extent that we no longer crave the approval of men and women. He desires for us to dress modestly and economically rather than arrogantly and expensively. He challenges us, even today: "Why spend [your] money on what is not bread, and your labor on what does not satisfy?" (Isa. 55:2 NIV).

Expensive fashions do not nourish us. Costly cosmetic surgeries and hair-implant procedures do not nurture us. They may draw attention and garner compliments, but they will never satisfy the longings of our hearts. If we "dress to impress" in order to gain the approval and respect of men and women, we are spending our money for things that do not satisfy.

Decency

When Paul wrote Timothy, he also urged "women to dress . . . with decency" (1 Tim. 2:9 NIV). Paul may have been writing his letter from Macedonia, perhaps even Corinth, a decadent city that was proud of its Temple of Aphrodite staffed by a thousand sacred prostitutes, who plied their indecent trade on the city's streets. In Ephesus, where Timothy ministered (see 1 Tim. 1:3), the Temple of Diana was staffed by hundreds of seductively dressed priestesses called the *Melissae* (which means "the bees") and eunuchs (called "drones"). In a culture that wore its sexuality on its sleeve, so to speak, Paul said their indecent fashions are not appropriate for women who profess to worship Christ.

Like Timothy and Paul, we live in a culture that seems to delight in revealing fashions and styles of dress that leave little to the imagination. If Paul were writing today, he might also have mentioned breast-enhancement surgery and "buttock implants." Beauty and fashion choices that inflame the interest and passion of anyone except our own husband or wife cross the lines of decency.

It is God's expressed desire for men and women who profess to follow Christ to pursue his standard of decency in our personal appearance, rather than the world's standards of youth, beauty, slimness, and fitness. Again, that's not to say those things are wrong in and of themselves but that our primary emphasis when we stand before the mirror should be modesty and decency, not looking "hot" or inflaming passions.

Propriety

The third principle of personal appearance Paul cited to Timothy was propriety. He specified that women should dress "with . . . propriety, not with braided hair or gold or pearls or expensive clothes" (1 Tim. 2:9 NIV).

New Testament scholar William Barclay points out that "in Greek society there were women whose whole life consisted in elaborate dressing and braiding of the hair. . . . Even the Greeks and the Romans were shocked at the love of dress and adornment which characterized some of their women."[4] In that context Paul wrote to Timothy, who was laboring in Ephesus, a center of Greek religion and culture. Paul's point isn't that braided hair and fine fashions are immoral in themselves but they cross the boundary of propriety. Propriety is a sense for what is appropriate, what is fitting for a specific situation. What is appropriate for the bedroom is not appropriate for the board room. What is appropriate for the beach is not appropriate for the street. What is appropriate among family is not always appropriate everywhere else.

President Ronald Reagan reportedly refused to enter the Oval Office during the eight years of his presidency without a coat and tie. He thought anything more casual would be inappropriate considering the dignity of the high office he held. That was a standard not of decency or modesty but of propriety.

Standards of propriety have blurred and all but disappeared in our culture these days. Some young women have taken to wearing lingerie to the office and pajamas to go jogging. Some young men will wear the same clothes to a job interview that they would wear to work out. Some folks forget that it's *always* proper to be clean and odor free! In such cases it's not primarily a question of modesty or even decency; the issue is propriety.

A concern for propriety can be tricky, because it can so easily cross the line into dressing to impress. The difference, however, becomes clearer when you realize that the person with a godly sense of propriety is seeking primarily to please God, not men. The goal is not to "look cool" and draw attention to oneself but to be appropriate and give glory to God.

Beauty

The final standard Paul urges on Timothy is a different kind of beauty, God's standard. Notice the last part of the passage:

> I . . . want women to dress modestly, with decency and propriety, not with braided hair or gold or pearls or expensive clothes, *but with good deeds, appropriate for women who profess to worship God.* (1 Tim. 2:9–10 NIV, italics added)

Paul says, "I want women to dress themselves with good deeds." That's the kind of apparel, the kind of fashion and beauty, that most attractively adorns the person who professes to worship God. And how like God it is: your beauty in his eyes doesn't depend on things outside your control (like good cheekbones or a creamy complexion) but on things entirely within your control (like mowing the lawn for an invalid or rocking a baby in the church nursery).

God is less interested in whether your nose or teeth are crooked than whether your actions are. He is far less impressed by a flattering hairdo than he is by the deeds you do. He is much less concerned with the makeup on your face than he is with the makeup of your character. He is much less pleased by your sculpted biceps than by your surrendered heart.

God doesn't want people to look at you and marvel at your youthful beauty; he wants people to look at you and worship him. He doesn't want people to ask how you stay in such good shape; he wants people to ask why your life is different. He doesn't want people to see you and ask for your plastic surgeon's name; he wants people to see you and glorify his name:

> Let your light shine before men, so that they may see
> your good deeds and give glory to your Father in
> heaven. (Matt. 5:16)

You may not always see these standards of modesty, decency, propriety, and (true) beauty in the church. You may not always see them on Christian television or among Christian performers. You certainly won't see them reflected in the world. But that's exactly why they are so powerful: because they are so rare. Men and women who apply God's standards for personal appearance and adorn themselves with good deeds instead of expensive clothes will reap a rich harvest (Gal. 6:9). And those of us who remove the idol of youth, beauty, slimness, and fitness from the altar of our hearts will open the way for God to work in us and through us in new and greater ways.

Objects Are Closer Than They Appear

If you're an American or have been touched by American culture, the chances are high that your attitudes about your personal appearance reflect the world around you more than the Holy Spirit inside you. It's likely that worldly standards of youth, beauty, slimness, and fitness occupy a much larger space in your heart than you've intended to give them. It's possible that they've even become idols to you, though you never intended for that to happen.

I encourage you to stop now and ask God if you've been treating your personal appearance (or even your supposed lack of youth, beauty, slimness, or physical fitness) as an idol. Ask him to reveal to you any ways that you have placed an ungodly emphasis on the world's priorities. You might ask him questions like these:

- Have I let the process of aging, my natural appearance, my weight, or my physical condition make me feel less acceptable to you?
- Do I feel an unhealthy pressure to be young, beautiful, slim, and fit?
- Have I spent an unhealthy amount of time, money, or attempts in my efforts to feel young, beautiful, slim, and fit?
- Have I been basing my sense of self-esteem on external qualities alone?
- Have I ever bragged about (or taken pride in) what an item of clothing or jewelry cost?
- Do I try to impress others with my physical appearance, or am I striving to please you?
- Are you happy with the amount of time I spend on my physical appearance as opposed to the amount of time I spend in your presence?
- Has my approach to my physical appearance reflected your priorities of modesty, decency, propriety, and beauty?
- Am I trying to obtain the praise of people for myself or for you?

It's possible, of course, to grow in all those areas, but if you are sincerely and patiently asking God such questions, he will reveal to you any idolatry that exists in your heart. He may show you one area in particular where you are prone to place an ungodly emphasis on appearance. He may disclose to you that your sorrow over not being "young enough," "beautiful enough," "slim enough," or "fit enough" in your own eyes or the eyes of others is a form of idolatry. He may expose to you ways in which your personal appearance does not reflect biblical standards of modesty, decency, propriety, and (true) beauty.

If he does any of those things, let me remind you to repent and, with God's help, turn from all idolatry of the heart. Pray for deliverance from all ungodly concern for your appearance and any ungodly emphasis on your physical appearance. Then let me suggest a spiritual exercise to help you cooperate with the Holy Spirit in changing your heart.

There are people in your life—women and men—who exemplify 1 Timothy 2:9–10. They epitomize a modest, decent, proper, and truly beautiful appearance. They adorn themselves not only modestly, decently, and properly but also with good deeds, appropriate for men and women who profess to worship God. As a means of disciplining your mind and spirit, take time to identify those people in your life, family, church, and community, and then thank them for their testimony to you of what it means to be beautiful in appearance (you may write a note, pay a visit, make a phone call, or simply approach the person after church or Bible study, for example).

Do this between seven and twenty-one times (research shows that it takes seven to twenty-one times for most of us to learn something and make it a part of us). Be careful, when you're thanking that person, to do so in a way that glorifies God, not in a way that promotes the same ungodly standards you're trying to cast down. For example, saying something like this: "God has really used you as an example to me of his standards for both inner and outer beauty. Thank you," will both bless the person and glorify God, whereas, "I just wish I could be as good-looking as you," does neither.

And, finally, as you observe this exercise, pray that God will use these real-life examples to create in you a clean heart and renew a right spirit that reflects his standards for your physical appearance, and not the world's standards.

> *God of beauty, God of all, I confess to you the ungodly ways that I focus on outward appearance, both mine and others', especially __(in this way)__. Please deliver me from all extremes, from all idolatrous tendencies to please men instead of you.*
>
> *Help me to seek your approval. Help me to bask in the knowledge that I am "remarkably and wonderfully made" (Ps. 139:14). Help me to learn what pleases you and to pursue modesty, decency, and propriety in how I appear to others that I might glorify you. And help me to clothe myself with good deeds that those around me might see me and glorify you, in Jesus' name, amen.*

THIRTEEN

The La-Z-Boy Life

You should see my friend's new car.

It boasts charcoal-colored leather seats that are not only beautiful to look at but oh, so comfortable to sit in. The contoured bucket seats in front feature adjustable lumbar support so the seat will conform to the shape of your body. Both front and rear seats are also heated, so on cold winter mornings you can toast your buns on the way to work. Oh, yeah, and the front seats are likewise ventilated: A fan in each seat draws air from between the seat and passenger's body through numerous small holes in the leather upholstery, creating an effect like a cool sea breeze on a sunny day. Such attention to comfort produces something like a spa experience in a car. And that's just the seats!

The car also offers four distinct climate zones for heating and cooling, which can be set to different temperatures. A computer automatically adjusts the airflow to ensure that each passenger enjoys the temperature he or she prefers. The car's interior humidity is automatically raised or lowered to increase comfort and prevent windows from fogging. And when a sensor in the car detects fumes from a belching diesel truck, a traffic tunnel, or a pig farm, it automatically closes the fresh air intake.

Add to that a premium sound system and satellite radio, mirrors that automatically adjust to daytime or nighttime, adjustable brake and gas pedals, and subtle but effective LEDs to illuminate all the buttons and controls on the dashboard, and you have the ultimate in automotive comfort. A lavish driving experience. And one that is quintessentially American.

The God of My Comfort

The Bible speaks favorably of comfort. God called out to Isaiah the prophet, "'Comfort, comfort My people,' says your God" (Isa. 40:1). And Paul, the great church planter, referred to our God as "the God of all comfort [who] comforts us in all our affliction, so that we may be able to comfort those who are in any kind of affliction, through the comfort we ourselves receive from God" (2 Cor. 1:3–4). That, of course, is the kind of comfort the dictionary defines as "to give strength and hope to" or "to ease the grief or trouble of."

But that's not the kind of comfort we are discussing. No, the kind of comfort we tend to idolize is the comfort my friend enjoyed in his car, the kind of comfort afforded by air conditioners and purifiers, plush seating, electronically adjustable beds, noise-cancelling headphones, home spas, and La-Z-Boy recliners.

That kind of comfort is an American ideal. Even when we're "roughing it," it seems. Take, for example, the following comments and suggestions which were submitted to the staff of Wyoming's Bridger Wilderness Area in 1996:

- Trails need to be reconstructed. Please avoid building trails that go uphill.
- Trails need to be wider so people can walk holding hands.
- Too many bugs and spiders and spiderwebs. Please spray the wilderness area to get rid of these pests.

- Please pave the trails so they can be plowed clear of snow in winter.
- Chairlifts need to be in some places so we can get to wonderful views without having to hike to them.
- The coyotes made too much noise last night and kept me awake. Please eradicate these annoying animals.
- A small deer came into my camp and stole my jar of pickles. Is there any way I can get reimbursed?
- Reflectors need to be placed on trees every fifty feet so people can hike at night with flashlights.
- Escalators would be good on steep uphill sections.
- A McDonald's would be nice at the trailhead.
- The places where trails do not exist are not well marked.
- Too many rocks in the mountains.[1]

I traveled recently with my lovely wife down the Pacific Coast Highway and visited San Simeon, the palatial "country estate" of William Randolph Hearst (which is now a California state historical monument). I was fascinated to learn that Hearst's father, a wealthy miner, purchased the land just off the Pacific in 1865 and called it "Camp Hill." For decades the family enjoyed its wilderness setting as a place to "rough it" on camping trips (though even these trips featured elaborate arrangements and separate sleeping and dining tents). But, in 1919, publisher Hearst wrote to famed San Francisco architect Julia Morgan, "Miss Morgan, we are tired of camping out in the open at the ranch in San Simeon and I would like to build a little something." The "little something" became an awe-inspiring, luxurious estate of 165 rooms and 127 acres of gardens, terraces, pools, and walkways. In one generation "Camp Hill" became "Hearst Castle," a ten-million-dollar parable of our worshipful pursuit of comfort.

Yeah, we like our comfort in America. More than that: we cherish it. We revere it. In fact, we are often like the Israelites of Amos's day: we worship not the God of all comfort but the god of *my* comfort.

The Idol: Comfort

Amos was a man who lived during the reigns of King Jeroboam II of the Northern Kingdom, Israel, and King Uzziah of Judah, the Southern Kingdom, at a time when both kingdoms were enjoying periods of prosperity. His hometown was Tekoa, near Bethlehem in Judah, where he worked as a shepherd. But sometime in 750 or 749 BC, he traveled to Bethel in the Northern Kingdom to deliver a message from God, which has been preserved to this day in the Old Testament book that bears his name.

In a mere day or two, Amos spoke what God had told him to say, and among his words were these, from the sixth chapter:

> Woe to those who are at ease in Zion
> and to those who feel secure on the hill of Samaria—
> the notable people in this first of the nations,
> those the house of Israel comes to. (Amos 6:1–2)

Amos promised "woe to God's people," pronouncing a scathing denunciation of them. Why? What was his problem? Was his ulcer acting up? Was it because his own life had been bitter and hard, and he resented their ease? Was it because he wanted in on the action, because he wanted a piece of the pie?

No. Amos was, of course, speaking at God's command. And he pronounced "woe" to those who were at ease in Zion and Samaria (the capitals of the Southern and Northern Kingdoms, respectively) because they were living in a fool's paradise. He addressed the "notable people in this first of the nations," the dignitaries and celebrities the common people looked to and consulted, the kind of folks who sat in the air-conditioned boxes in the sports stadium and cut ribbons at dedication ceremonies, and he pronounced God's judgment on their comfort and ease.

> Cross over to Calneh and see;
> go from there to great Hamath;
> then go down to Gath of the Philistines.
> Are you better than these kingdoms?
> Is their territory larger than yours?

You dismiss any thought of the evil day
and bring in a reign of violence. (Amos 6:2–3)

He mentions fine cities that were once like Zion and Samaria, sitting on top of the world, enjoying a booming economy, living in the lap of luxury until misfortune swept in on them and left them in ruins. Calneh, Hamath, and Gath had all been conquered by the Assyrians, the superpower to the east.

"Are you better than they?" he asks. "Do you think they were not at ease in their homes and palaces, too?"

Then, apparently, Amos points the finger at those living in comfort and ease, and says:

> They lie on beds inlaid with ivory,
> sprawled out on their couches,
> and dine on lambs from the flock
> and calves from the stall.
> They improvise songs to the sound of the harp
> and invent their own musical instruments like David.
> They drink wine by the bowlful
> and anoint themselves with the finest oils
> but do not grieve over the ruin of Joseph.
> Therefore, they will now go into exile
> as the first of the captives,
> and the feasting of those who sprawl out
> will come to an end. (Amos 6:4–7)

They had it good. They enjoyed every delicacy. As a culture, as a nation, and as individuals, they sat at the top of the economic heap. Sort of like Westerners in general, and Americans in particular. If Amos were writing today, he might say:

> They lie in adjustable beds with memory foam
>   mattresses and advanced contour pillow features
>   sprawled out in their Barcaloungers and La-Z-Boys,
>   and dine on made-to-order meals cooked just right
>   and pizzas delivered to their door.
> They revel in their high-definition plasma-screen TVs
>   and their surround-sound stereo systems.

> They drink lattes and cappuccinos by the urnful
> and luxuriate in home Jacuzzis
> and under pulsating showerheads
> but do not grieve over the things that break God's
> heart.

But hold on just a minute. There's nothing wrong with a nice Starbucks latte or a pulsating showerhead. What's the problem?

The problem, for us as it was for Israel and Judah in Amos's day, is not that we have a few comforts. The problem is that our comforts have us.

The Problem: Complacency

When Amos, under God's inspiration, pronounced "woe" to those who were at ease in Zion and Samaria, he was not complaining that they drank wine or improvised songs. He was not condemning the people for their fancy beds or meals of lamb. He condemned them for turning ease into complacency and comfort into an idol.

So it is with us. I happen to like my recliner as much as anyone, but I must admit that somewhere along the line, I have come to expect comfort, cherish it, even demand it. And I know I'm not alone. Many Americans, who sincerely claim to follow Christ, think twice about attending church when the weather is bad or even threatening. We opt out of Easter sunrise services because they happen so early. Some of us even select a church because they serve coffee or have comfortable seats.

Now, don't get me wrong. I like coffee and comfortable seats, and I'm no fan of the church pew (I secretly doubt that hard wood pews were invented by a godly person, perhaps not even a decent person). And I happen to believe there's absolutely nothing wrong with four-inch padding and cupholders in church sanctuary seating, especially if it's a church that strives to be hospitable to skeptics and seekers, folks who aren't yet Christ followers.

But we go too far to expect, or demand, comfort. We go too far when our expectations of comfort drive our choices, our worship, our service. Comfort becomes an idol when it prevents me from hearing God and doing what he calls me to do. Comfort is an idol when it shapes how I respond to God instead of God shaping how I respond to comfort. Comfort is an idol when it shapes my expectations of what it means to be spiritual, to be Christian.

Princeton University sociologist Robert Wuthnow writes:

> At one time theologians argued that the chief purpose of humankind was to glorify God. Now it would seem that the logic has been reversed: the chief purpose of God is to glorify humankind. Spirituality no longer is true or good because it meets absolute standards of truth or goodness, but because it helps me get along. I am the judge of its worth. If it helps me find a vacant parking space, I know my spirituality is on the right track. If it leads me into the wilderness, calling me to face dangers I would rather not deal with at all, then it is a form of spirituality I am unlikely to choose.[2]

We are so accustomed to comfort that when our spiritual life hits a snag, or our commitment to Christ costs us something, we panic and wonder what went wrong. But God never promised an easy, comfortable life. Nowhere in the Bible does it say we will be appreciated and understood. Nowhere did Jesus tell us to expect our relationships with others to be smooth and trouble-free. It doesn't say our expectations will all be met. Actually it says the very opposite:

> You will have suffering in this world. Be courageous! (John 16:33)

> Endure hardship with us as a good soldier of Christ Jesus. (2 Tim. 2:3 NIV)

> All those who want to live a godly life in Christ Jesus will be persecuted. (2 Tim. 3:12)

> Consider it a great joy, my brothers, whenever you experience various trials, knowing that the testing of your faith produces endurance. But endurance must do its

complete work, so that you may be mature and
complete, lacking nothing. (James 1:2–4)

Judging from what we see in the Word of God, comfort is
not a common experience of men and women who are committed to God. Certainly not Jesus, who didn't even consider the
pain and shame of death on a cross too much for his Father to
ask (Heb. 12:2). Certainly not Paul, who endured . . .

> . . . labors,
> . . . imprisonments,
> . . . beatings, near death many times.
> Five times I received from the Jews 40 lashes minus one.
> Three times I was beaten with rods.
> Once I was stoned.
> Three times I was shipwrecked.
> I have spent a night and a day
>   in the depths of the sea.
> On frequent journeys, I faced
> dangers from rivers, dangers from robbers,
> dangers from my own people,
>   dangers from the Gentiles,
> dangers in the city,
>   dangers in the open country,
> dangers on the sea, and dangers
>   among false brothers;
> labors and hardship,
> many sleepless nights,
>   hunger and thirst,
> often without food, cold,
>   and lacking clothing.
> Not to mention other things. . . . (2 Cor. 11:23b–28a)

When the news reached the United States in 1955 that Jim
Elliot and four other missionaries had been speared to death by a
remote tribe of South American natives they had been ministering to, many Christians, including those men's families, stepped
forward to volunteer for the mission field, feeling called to fill
those men's shoes. But that was then; this is now. Would that be

the American church's response today? Would we go? Or would we remain at ease in Zion?

The Prescription: Sacrifice

Amos rebuked the people of Zion and Samaria for their allegiance to comfort and their complacency toward the things that were breaking God's heart. Notice especially the italicized phrase below:

> They lie on beds inlaid with ivory,
> sprawled out on their couches,
> and dine on lambs from the flock
> and calves from the stall.
> They improvise songs to the sound of the harp
> and invent their own musical instruments like David.
> They drink wine by the bowlful
> and anoint themselves with the finest oils
> *but do not grieve over the ruin of Joseph.*
> Therefore, they will now go into exile
> as the first of the captives,
> and the feasting of those who sprawl out
> will come to an end. (Amos 6:4–7, emphasis added)

"They do not grieve over the ruin of Joseph," Amos says, using a synonym for the people of God. The people of Israel and Judah were careful and attentive to serve the proper wine with fish, but they were careless of the moral decline of their nation. They spent time and thought on the furnishings for their homes but thought nothing of the need for spiritual revival among the people of God. Their comfort was all that concerned them.

"They do not grieve over the ruin of Joseph." They stay in their cozy small group because it's so comfortable, while folks around them are starving for community. They neglect the prayer opportunities their church offers because they're not "comfortable" praying in front of other people. They write checks for others to go on mission trips and service projects but don't go themselves because those places make them uncomfortable.

"They do not grieve over the ruin of Joseph." They measure their witness to a dying world against their "comfort level." They worship in ways they're "comfortable" with. They give amounts they're comfortable giving. They resign or stop attending or change churches when someone threatens their comfort. Because their comfort is their god.

Our exaltation of comfort is really a failure to trust God. Do I really believe that he is in control? Do I really believe he knows what he's doing? Do I really believe he knows what is best for me? Do I believe that if I put him in the driver's seat he will not hurt me? Do I believe that if I deny myself and sacrifice my own comfort that he will take care of me? Do I believe that his will is better than my own comfort? Do I believe that what he wants out of me is more important than what I want (or think I want) out of life? Do I mean it when I pray, "Thy will be done?"

Rejecting the La-Z-Boy Life

Comfort feels better than suffering. "Nice" feels better than "not nice." Ease feels better than self-denial and sacrifice.

But God's favor is better than life itself (Ps. 63:3). A day in his presence is better than a thousand elsewhere (Ps. 84:10). And no amount of physical or emotional comfort can compensate for losing his hand of blessing on our lives.

So how do we reject the La-Z-Boy life? How do we resist the idol of comfort? How do we replace it with a renewed faith in the one true God?

Repent

As I've said before, of course, there is only one way to correct idolatry, and that is simply and completely to repent of it. Get thoroughly and brutally honest with yourself. Ask God to reveal to you the full extent of your idolatry and faithlessness in this area, so he can heal you. Ask him:

- In what ways have I chosen comfort over your commands and plans for my life?
- What choices have I made purely for comfort's sake? Were any of them contrary to your will?
- Whom have I neglected or avoided because it would be uncomfortable for me?
- Have you been calling me to any service or ministry that I have been slow to hear because of my discomfort with the idea?
- Have I been exalting my "comfort level" over the needs of others?
- Have I given to you only what I'm comfortable giving?
- Have I come to expect my discipleship path to be an easy one?
- Have I been keeping you out of the driver's seat because of a preference for things I'm comfortable with?

Ask him those things and then listen for his answer. In fact, ask him to suggest other questions to you that aren't on the list above. Ask him to shine his searchlight into your heart and mind and reveal any idolatry to you, so you may confess it and turn from it.

"Take words with you," as Hosea pleaded, "and return to the LORD. Say to him, 'Forgive all [my] sins and receive [me] graciously'" (Hos. 14:2 NIV). That is the first step.

Resist

Once you have repented, the next step is to add your actions to your intentions. The only antidote to the idol of comfort is self-denial and sacrifice. Jesus said:

> Anyone who intends to come with me has to let me
> lead. You're not in the driver's seat; I am. Don't run
> from suffering; embrace it. Follow me and I'll show you
> how. (Matt. 16:24 *The Message*)

The idol of comfort must be resisted with prayerful, conscious, concerted efforts. And the focus of those efforts must be sacrificial service. The author of the book of Hebrews wrote:

> Jesus . . . suffered outside the gate, so that He might sanctify the people by His own blood. Let us then go to Him outside the camp, bearing His disgrace. For here we do not have an enduring city; instead, we seek the one to come. Therefore, through Him let us continually offer up to God a sacrifice of praise, that is, the fruit of our lips that confess His name. Don't neglect to do good and to share, for God is pleased with such sacrifices. (Heb. 13:12–16)

Following Jesus' example of sacrificing comfort for the benefit of others, choose at least one of the following ways "to do good and to share," praying as you do that God will use your spiritual exercise to deliver you from an idolatrous attachment to comfort:

- Get your hands dirty; volunteer in a soup kitchen, church mission, or some other practical place of service where comfort is at a premium.
- Step out of your comfort zone, something that would set apart God in your heart by exalting him and reminding you that he is more important than your own comfort (sharing your spiritual story with someone on the bus, for example, or chaperoning a youth group trip, etc.).
- Sign up for a mission trip to a foreign country or inner-city mission, or practice self-denial (sacrificing some personal comfort to benefit missions, such as walking instead of driving and donating the savings to missions).

Replace

The writer to the Hebrews said, "Let us continually offer up to God a sacrifice of praise, that is, the fruit of our lips that confess His name" (Heb. 13:15).

If your heart has been in the habit of lifting up your own comfort in an idolatrous way, then the third thing you must do is to redouble all efforts to replace that false god with the true God in your affections and allegiance. Renew your personal worship and prayer habits. Seek every opportunity to "offer up to God a sacrifice of praise" (v. 15). Strive to focus your heart and mind so fully on God that there will be less and less room for the idol of comfort.

One way to do that is with daily affirmations of faith in the true God, especially affirmations that will counter any tendencies that gave rise to the exaltation of comfort in the first place. For example, you might once daily recite the following:

> *Lord God, I believe that you are in control.*
> *I believe you know what you're doing.*
> *I believe you know what is best for me.*
> *I believe that if I put you in the driver's seat you will*
>   *not hurt me.*
> *I believe that if I deny myself and sacrifice my own*
>   *comfort, you will take care of me.*
> *I believe that your will is far better than my own comfort.*
> *I believe that what you want out of me is more important*
>   *than what I want (or think I want) out of life.*
> *Lord God, I believe in you.*

Feel free to create your own series of affirmations, focusing on areas that will help you replace your faith in the false god of comfort with a real, strong, daily faith in the one true God. Consider printing them onto a bookmark, mouse pad, or refrigerator magnet. Ask your accountability partner to help you make such affirmations a habit. Repeat them as often as necessary and for as long as necessary until you and others start to recognize the fruit of your repentance and faith in your life.

> *God, I confess that I value my own comfort too highly, and*
> *sometimes exalt my own comfort above your commands and*
> *plans for my life, especially when I _____. I confess*
> *that I don't believe in you as I should. But I want to.*

Help me to believe that you are in control. Help me believe that you know what you're doing. Help me believe that you know what is best for me. Help me believe that if I put you in the driver's seat you will not hurt me. Help me believe that if I deny myself and sacrifice my own comfort, you will take care of me. Help me believe that your will is far better than my own comfort. Help me believe that what you want out of me is more important than what I want (or think I want) out of life.

Please teach me to be more and more like your Son, "who for the joy that lay before Him endured a cross and despised the shame" (Heb. 12:2), denying himself and sacrificing himself for my salvation and my eternal good. Teach me to endure hardship as a good soldier of Christ Jesus (see 2 Tim. 2:3) and to consider it a great joy whenever I experience trials, knowing that the testing of my faith produces endurance. Let endurance do its complete work in me so that I may be mature and complete, lacking nothing (see James 1:2–4), in Jesus' name, amen.

FOURTEEN

The Modern Baal

A friend and I were talking on my front porch one day. He is always an animated speaker. But on this occasion, though we had been having a lively conversation, his eyes widened and sparkled when the subject of his retirement fund came up.

He told me that he had bought shares in a technology-oriented mutual fund a year or two before, and his money had more than tripled!

"I've been pumping as much money into it as I can spare," he said. "It's amazing! If it keeps going like this, I'll be able to retire early!"

It didn't keep going like that, of course. As you can probably guess, my friend's story ended in near disaster. The fund, which had grown exponentially in 1999 and early 2000, met a grisly fate when the so-called "Dot Com Bubble" burst in mid-2000. My friend's growing fortune not only stopped growing; it declined in value until, at least for awhile, his stake was worth less than the original amounts he had invested.

He wasn't alone, of course. Many investors had their hearts broken that year, and many others have learned the perils of the stock market in the years since. Including me.

I've thought about that conversation many times since then. I remember the contagious glimmer in my friend's eyes. I recall his obvious enthusiasm when talking about his investment success. I can easily recollect my own emotions at the time: happiness for him, along with more than a little envy, and a desire for some of the action.

As I reflect, I can't avoid the conclusion that we were both flirting with, perhaps even bowing to, an idol. I say "perhaps" because I don't want to cast aspersions on my friend. But I know my own heart. I am an idolater.

Dangerous Commodity

"Those who want to be rich," Paul told Timothy, "fall into temptation, a trap, and many foolish and harmful desires, which plunge people into ruin and destruction. For the love of money is a root of all kinds of evil, and by craving it, some have wandered away from the faith and pierced themselves with many pains" (1 Tim. 6:9–10).

Money is a dangerous commodity. Not neutral. Dangerous. Those who crave it, those who hoard it, and those who put their faith in it place their spiritual life in jeopardy and set themselves up for disappointment and disaster.

James the apostle wrote:

> Come now, you rich people! Weep and wail over the
> miseries that are coming on you. Your wealth is ruined;
> your clothes are moth-eaten; your silver and gold are
> corroded, and their corrosion will be a witness against
> you and will eat your flesh like fire. You stored up treas-
> ure in the last days! Look! The pay that you withheld
> from the workers who reaped your fields cries out, and
> the outcry of the harvesters has reached the ears of the

> Lord of Hosts. You have lived luxuriously on the land
> and have indulged yourselves. You have fattened your
> hearts for the day of slaughter. You have condemned—
> you have murdered—the righteous man; he does not
> resist you. (James 5:1–6)

Wow, James, how about saying what you *really* think? Those
are pretty forceful words. Pretty uncompromising. But, then,
James was never one to mince words, so we should not be surprised that, writing under the inspiration of God's Holy Spirit, he
agrees with Paul and identifies three dangers of money.

Corrosion

James's words in that passage above bring to mind the words
of Jesus, who said:

> Don't collect for yourselves treasures on earth, where
> moth and rust destroy and where thieves break in and
> steal. But collect for yourselves treasures in heaven,
> where neither moth nor rust destroys, and where thieves
> don't break in and steal. (Matt. 6:19–20)

Jesus and James are clearly both singing from the Holy Spirit's
song sheet, so to speak. They both identify the fact that money
tends to corrode, and the best earthly investments can slip through
your fingers. The more you have, the more you stand to lose.

Jesus advises us to collect treasure in heaven instead of
hoarding it here on earth, and James admonishes:

> You have hoarded wealth in the last days. (James 5:3 NIV)

It is unspeakably dangerous to hoard wealth in the last days,
the time of history when at any moment the King of glory, Jesus
the risen one, may return, and the time for repentance will be
past. There is no worse time to hoard wealth than the end of days,
when time grows short, when wealth could have been invested to
expand the kingdom of God and spent to bring hurting men and
women into the knowledge of the grace and healing that is found
only through faith in Jesus Christ.

Wealth tends to corrode. Thus, the man or woman who hoards it—like the one-talent servant in Jesus' parable of the talents, who buried his master's money while his peers invested their trust funds for their master's benefit—is gambling not only with money but also with the lives and souls of hurting, wandering, lost people all around them.

Corruption

James also says to the wealthy: "Look! The wages you failed to pay the workmen who mowed your fields are crying out against you. The cries of the harvesters have reached the ears of the Lord Almighty" (James 5:4 NIV). James is not saying it is a sin to be rich. He's saying, wealth tends to corrupt.

Two businessmen were comparing notes down on Miami Beach.

"I'm here on insurance money," one said. "I collected $50,000 for fire damage to my business."

"Me too," the other said. "But I got $100,000 for flood damage."

After a long pause, the first man said, "How do you start a flood?"

It's not a matter of what you have but what has you. And "those who want to be rich fall into temptation, a trap, and many foolish and harmful desires, which plunge people into ruin and destruction" (1 Tim. 6:9).

Jesus said: "For where your treasure is, there your heart will be also" (Matt. 6:21).

Those words ought to terrify many of us who say we follow Jesus. We tend to misread Jesus' words, as if he said, "For where your heart is, there your treasure will be also." But that's not what he said. He said our heart will "follow the money." Its lure is that strong; its power is that irresistible.

J. R. R. Tolkien's *Lord of the Rings* fantasy offers a vivid illustration for us. One of the characters in the story is a pitiful, loathsome creature named Gollum. As the story unfolds, however, we learn that he was once no different from Frodo, Sam, and Pippin, the hobbit heroes of the story. But he found a magical ring. He kept it. He hoarded it. He began to call it "Precious." Until one day Gollum no longer owned the ring; the ring owned him.

Money is not neutral. It can be used for good or evil, but it is a dangerous commodity because it tends to corrupt, leading the way for the heart to follow.

Complacency

James also said: "You have lived on earth in luxury and self-indulgence. You have fattened yourselves in the day of slaughter" (James 5:5 NIV).

Have you ever sat on a cruise ship, soaked in a Jacuzzi, or ridden in a fancy car, and said, "I could get used to this!" That's what James is talking about.

James says, when we are not content to have our basic needs provided (see 1 Tim. 6:8) but go on stuffing our pockets, filling our bank accounts, enlarging our garages, plumping up our bottom line, adding to our net worth, we are like a cow stopping to fill its belly with more fodder on the way to the slaughterhouse. We are ignoring (or disbelieving) the shortness of time we have on this earth compared to the eternal reward that awaits us. We are mortgaging our heavenly rewards in order to live in luxury on this side of eternity.

As a bell ringer for the Salvation Army's red kettle campaign every Christmas, I can testify that the people in the finest clothes and fanciest cars tend to display less generosity than folks who don't appear to have much money. My daughter, who worked her way through college as a server in various restaurants, has similarly observed that her wealthiest patrons are among the least likely to leave a generous tip. And research shows that the percentage of income people give to church and charity declines steadily as their wealth increases.

One of the great dangers of money is that it breeds complacency. For some of us, money acts on our consciences like the L-tryptophan in turkey acts on our bodies; the more bloated we become, the less energy we can summon.

Money is dangerous. But for some of us—particularly Americans, it seems—it becomes more than a dangerous commodity; it becomes a deadly idol, a modern Baal.

Then and Now

Back in the days of the exodus, and later in the days of the prophet Samuel, and still later in the time of Elijah and beyond, there was a prominent and pervasive form of idol worship known as "Baalism." Baal was a god of the Canaanites, whose land Israel conquered. But there's far more to the story than that.

The Hebrew word *baal* means simply "lord" or "master" (even "husband," in some cases). It was the name not only of the primary Canaanite deity but also the god of Tyre (who was also called Melqart), the god of Mount Peor, and the god of the Akkadians (also called Hadad).

This god, Baal, could be found nearly everywhere in ancient society in one form or another. He seemed easily to infiltrate differing cultures, including Israelite culture. Baal worship seemed to hold on stubbornly and return regularly in spite of frequent and courageous attempts to expel him.

In these respects Baal (the false god of ancient Canaan) is much like money, a modern American idol. This idol takes many forms—not only dollars, but also gold, silver, yen, pounds, francs, deutsche marks, and more. It is pervasive: one needs only to read *The Wall Street Journal* or *Fortune* magazine; scan the daily stories of merger, scandal, and economic conquest; read the ads promising strong yields, quick returns, and fail-safe schemes; attend the gatherings promising a piece of the action. And this modern Baal has infiltrated the church itself, where it holds on stubbornly and returns easily, despite efforts to expel it.

When Jesus said, in the Sermon on the Mount, "You cannot be slaves of God and of money" (Matt. 6:24), he could have used a half dozen Greek words for money:

> *argurion* (Matt. 25:18, 27; Luke 9:3)
> *chrema* (Acts 4:37; 8:18, 20)
> *chalkos* (Mark 6:8; 12:41)
> *stater* (Matt. 17:27)
> *nomisma* (Matt. 22:19)
> *philarguria* (1 Tim. 6:10)

But he used none of those terms. Instead, he used the word *mammonas* or *mammon*. That single word puts his comment in a different light. Richard Foster writes:

> When Jesus uses the Aramaic term mammon to refer to wealth, he is giving it a personal and spiritual character. When he declares, "You cannot serve God and mammon" (Matt. 6:24), he is personifying mammon as a rival god.[1]

"Well," you may say to yourself, "that's interesting enough, but I settled that issue and chose my priorities long ago. I serve God. Mammon isn't a problem for me."

Not so fast. When Jesus issued his warning about serving mammon, he was speaking to fellow Jews, God's people, folks who worshipped the one true God. Many in the crowd had already become Christ followers. Some in the crowd were dirt-poor by our standards. And yet Jesus warned them, "You cannot serve God and mammon" (Matt. 6:24 NKJV).

You may have become a Christ follower years ago. You may be a devoted church member. You may even tithe to your church and give generously to missions and charities. But that doesn't mean the modern Baal of money worship has no place in your life, no influence over you. As that great theologian Mark Twain wrote, "Some men worship rank, some worship heroes, some worship power, some worship God, and over these ideals they dispute and cannot unite—but they all worship money."[2]

So how can you know? How can you tell if you're prone to this modern American idol? How can you determine if you're flirting with or bowing to the idol Jesus called "mammon"? Allow me to suggest four indicators.

When Money Prevents Full Devotion

A young man once came to Jesus. He had heard of Jesus long before and had several times walked a great distance to hear him teach. He saw Jesus lay hands on little children and bless them. Finally, the opportunity presented itself, and the man shouldered his way through the crowd until he stood before the Man from Galilee.

"Good Teacher," he said, impulsively kneeling in the dust at Jesus' feet, "what must I do to inherit eternal life?"

Jesus leveled a long gaze at the man, noting by his expensive robes that he was not only an observant Jew but also a man of means. "Why do you call Me good?" Jesus asked him, the hint of a smile turning up the corners of his mouth. "No one is good but One—God."

The young man blinked but said nothing. Jesus continued.

"You know the commandments: Do not murder; do not commit adultery; do not steal; do not bear false witness; do not defraud; honor your father and mother."

"Teacher," the man said, his eyes sparkling with hope, "I have kept all these from my youth."

Jesus found his heart warming with compassion and affection for this earnest young man. "You lack one thing," he answered. "Go, sell all you have and give to the poor, and you will have treasure in heaven." He reached for the man's arm and lifted him to his feet and peered meaningfully into his eyes. "Then come, follow Me."

The two men locked gazes for a moment. But then, the young man dropped his gaze. He hesitated.

> A leaden moment passed between them, and finally the
> young man turned and walked through the suddenly
> parted crowd.[3]

That young man received the same call to follow Jesus as
Matthew, Andrew, Peter, and Phillip. He might have become one
of the Twelve. His name might have become as renowned as
Peter, James, and John. But he turned away, the Bible records,
"because he was very rich" (Luke 18:23).

Gordon MacDonald explains:

> Why did Jesus confront this young man about his wealth
> when others in the Bible (in both Old and New
> Testaments) appeared to be free to have many
> possessions?
>   The only conceivable answer is this: Jesus, looking
> into the other's heart, knew that the heart of this young
> man had been possessed by his own wealth. This rich
> young man defined himself with his money and his sta-
> tus. To put it another way, his money and his lifestyle
> were his gods, and he worshiped them both.[4]

Money is an idol if it prevents a full and fervent devotion to
God. And often it does. After the young man turned away, Jesus
mused to his followers, "How hard it is for those who have wealth
to enter the kingdom of God! For it is easier for a camel to go
through the eye of a needle than for a rich person to enter the
kingdom of God" (Luke 18:24–25).

Richard Foster points out:

> Note that when this young man went away sorrowful
> Jesus did not run after him and suggest that he only
> meant [his instruction] metaphorically, that all that was
> really required was a tithe. No, money had become an
> all-consuming idol, and it had to be rejected totally.[5]

As Dietrich Bonhoeffer has said, "Our hearts have room
only for one all-embracing devotion, and we can only cleave to
one Lord."[6] We cannot serve both God and mammon. If
money—its pursuit, its protection, or its proliferation—prevents

an all-embracing devotion to God, we are cleaving to an idol, a modern Baal.

When Money Projects a False Impression

Things were going so well.

The fledgling church in Jerusalem was thriving and growing, even in the midst of persecution. A spirit of excitement, community, and generosity characterized the church:

> Now the multitude of those who believed were of one heart and soul, and no one said that any of his possessions was his own, but instead, they held everything in common. And . . . there was not a needy person among them, because all those who owned lands or houses sold them, brought the proceeds of the things that were sold, and laid them at the apostles' feet. This was then distributed to each person as anyone had a need.
>
> Joseph, a Levite and a Cypriot by birth, whom the apostles named Barnabas, which is translated Son of Encouragement, sold a field he owned, brought the money, and laid it at the apostles' feet. (Acts 4:32–37)

Cool, huh? Apparently, everyone thought so because other folks started catching the fever, so to speak, from Barnabas. A married couple named Ananias and Sapphira also sold a piece of property. But they weren't as interested in giving as they were in receiving. They probably saw the admiration Barnabas received for his generosity, and they wanted some of the action. They also apparently wanted to appear more generous than they actually were. They may have intended to appear *more* generous than Barnabas.

In any case, the Bible says Ananias "kept back part of the proceeds with his wife's knowledge, and brought a portion of it and laid it at the apostle's feet" (Acts 5:2).

> Then Peter said, "Ananias, why has Satan filled your heart to lie to the Holy Spirit and keep back part of the proceeds from the field? Wasn't it yours while you

> possessed it? And after it was sold, wasn't it at your dis-
> posal? Why is it that you planned this thing in your
> heart? You have not lied to men but to God!" When he
> heard these words, Ananias dropped dead, and a great
> fear came on all who heard. (Acts 5:3–5)

I guess so! I don't know about you, but that would definitely
freak me out. In fact, not only did Ananias never get to enjoy the
tax deduction from his "donation," but his wife met the same fate
just three hours later (Acts 5:7–10).

Peter made it clear. Their sin wasn't donating some instead of
all of the proceeds; it was lying about it. Their actions betrayed
their true values: they were using money to create a false impression, to make themselves appear generous when in reality they
were making a cynical investment, trading money for reputation.

This is always an indication of idolatry. I once read that doc-
tors and lawyers tend to make great sums of money year after year
without gaining wealth (or giving away much of their income).[7]
Why? Because they feel compelled to create a certain impression
by driving expensive cars and living in expensive neighborhoods.
You don't have to be a millionaire to idolize money; you may
instead be duplicating Ananias and Sapphira's sin of using money
to project a false impression.

This may have been the downfall of King Hezekiah of Judah.
Hezekiah had sparked a spiritual revival in his kingdom, enjoyed a
miraculous victory over King Sennacherib of Assyria, and even
been healed of a fatal illness in answer to prayer. But his story in
the Old Testament ends badly, nonetheless. When Sennacherib's
successor heard about Hezekiah's healing, he sent envoys to
Jerusalem. Hezekiah "showed them his treasure house—the silver,
the gold, the spices, and the precious oil—and all his armory, and
everything that was found in his treasuries. There was nothing in
his palace . . . that Hezekiah did not show them" (Isa. 39:2).

When Isaiah the prophet learned what Hezekiah had done, he
delivered a rebuke, and the account in 2 Chronicles says that
God left Hezekiah (2 Chron. 32:30). What went wrong? It's not

completely clear, but I have a guess. I suspect that Hezekiah's "Magical Treasury Tour" was an effort to create an impression of wealth and glory on the foreign emissaries, one they were sure to take back to their king. But it was a false impression because Hezekiah's wealth, like ours, came from God and belonged to God.

When we use money to give other people the impression that we are successful, smart, or important, we become idolaters. When we give others the impression that our wealth came from us and belongs to us, we are denying God and exalting a modern Baal in his place.

When Money Promotes a Flawed Perspective

The news spread quickly as Jesus and his disciples approached the oasis of Jericho. Long before the thirteen men entered the town, they were surrounded by a crowd. Jesus' fame had grown, and he was greeted like a celebrity.

As they walked the narrow lane to the center of town, a short man in elegant attire frantically pursued them, seeking now and then to pierce the crowd around the teacher. But most were too intent on watching Jesus to notice him, and those that did notice intentionally boxed him out. He was the chief tax collector, and his fine home had been built by bribes and extortion.

But then the clever little man saw his opportunity. The mob would soon pass the sprawling sycamore tree near the center of town. He dashed ahead and clambered into the tree just in time to see Jesus before he passed by.

The famous Teacher from Galilee stopped and lifted his gaze. "Zacchaeus," he said. "Hurry and come down, because today I must stay at your house."

The tax collector froze for a moment, amazed at the use of his name, then quickly descended. Bowing and stammering, he led the way for Jesus and the Twelve to follow him to his home. He received Jesus like a king and listened raptly as he talked. His heart throbbed with something new—maybe it was hope, maybe faith, maybe even new life—as the Teacher gazed on him and spoke to him.

When Zacchaeus heard some of the guests from the town murmuring about Jesus eating in the home of such a sinner, he blurted, "Look, I'll give half of my possessions to the poor, Lord!" Even as he said the words, Zacchaeus himself was amazed that he meant them. "And if I have extorted anything from anyone, I'll pay back four times as much!"

Jesus studied the man for a moment before speaking. When he did speak, his words warmed the whole house. "Today," he said, "salvation has come to this house."

As Luke the historian records it (Luke 19:1–10), the evidence of Zacchaeus's salvation was a redeemed perspective of money! It would not be too much of a stretch to imagine that Zacchaeus traded gods that day, surrendering his former worship of money for a new devotion to Jesus Christ.

Unfortunately, that is too seldom the case. More often our flirtation with (or allegiance to) the idol of mammon is revealed in a flawed perspective. Richard Foster writes:

> [It is a distortion to believe] that money is a sign of God's blessing, and hence poverty is a sign of God's displeasure. This has been turned into a religion of personal peace and prosperity: crudely stated, "Love Jesus and get rich." Many churches are saturated with readily available gimmicks for blessedness, all the way from exact mathematical formulas (God will bless you sevenfold) to much more subtle but equally destructive forms.[8]

For example, we believe that the worth of those around us is measured by their income. (Foster points out that we are sometimes so bold as to ask questions like, "How much do you think she earns?" or "How much is he worth?") We equate God's values with the world's values (since "money makes the world go 'round," we think, and many preachers actually preach that "God wants me to be wealthy"). We apply faulty logic to God's Word instead of applying God's Word to our faulty logic, asking such things as, "Why would He (God) want all of *His* people poverty stricken while all of the people that aren't living for God have everything?"[9]

When the lack (or surplus) of money in our lives starts producing such flawed perspectives, we should be alert to the likelihood that we are entering the dangerous precincts of a modern idol.

When Money Persuades a Final Decision

A warning is in order here. It is extremely likely that the following paragraphs will step on your toes, perhaps worse. But one of the most rampant forms of idolatry in the world and the church today is a tendency (or, more accurately, a habit) of letting money rather than God guide our decisions.

James wrote:

> Look here, you people who say, "Today or tomorrow we are going to a certain town and will stay there a year. We will do business there and make a profit." How do you know what will happen tomorrow? For your life is like the morning fog—it's here a little while, then it's gone. What you ought to say is, "If the Lord wants us to, we will live and do this or that." (James 4:13–15 NLT).

That's just not how we do it, is it? No, our decision-making process more often sounds like, "I'd like to help, but we're really strapped this month," or "I sure hope our tax refund is enough to buy a new refrigerator." For most of us, most of the time, money persuades our decisions.

But, of course, this is not how things ought to be. Richard Foster again supplies keen insight:

> The Christian is given the high calling of *using* mammon without *serving* mammon. We are using mammon when we allow God to determine our economic

decisions. We are serving mammon when we allow mammon to determine our economic decisions. We simply must decide who is going to make our economic decisions—God or mammon.

Do we buy a particular home on the basis of the call of God, or because of the availability of money? Do we buy a new car because we can afford it, or because God instructed us to buy a new car? If money determines what we do or do not do, then money is our boss. If God determines what we do or do not do, then God is our boss. . . .

Suppose [my wife] Carolynn says to me, "Let's do this or that," and I complain, "But we don't have enough money!" What has happened? Money decided. You see, I did not say, "Well, honey, let's pray together and see if God wants us to do it." No, money made the decision. Money is my master. I am serving money.[10]

Our financial resources are, of course, a factor that can certainly be weighed in the decision-making process. Jesus acknowledged the common sense of sitting down and calculating the cost of a project or decision (Luke 14:28–30). But it should not rule the decision-making process, and money alone should not be the deciding factor because when it is, we are serving an idol.

A Modern Mount Carmel

The modern Baal—money, or "mammon," as Jesus called it—is a persistent, pervasive, and perilous idol. And like the Baal of Elijah's day, this idol will not easily be cast down.

First Kings 18 records the showdown between the prophet of God and the prophets of Baal. Elijah stood alone on Mount Carmel against 450 prophets of Baal and 400 prophets of Asherah. There the heavily outnumbered man of God challenged the Baal-worshippers to a duel. Each of them would erect an altar and prepare a bull on it but not kindle the fire. Then, Elijah said, "You call on the name of your god, and I will call on the name of Yahweh. The God who answers with fire, He is God" (1 Kings 18:24a).

The idolaters danced, wailed, and even mutilated themselves in a frantic, futile show. At the end of the day, their efforts had produced nothing but exhaustion.

Then Elijah took over and, confident in God's power, had them douse the offering three times until water filled even the trench around the altar. Then he prayed. And the fire came and consumed the offering, the wood, the altar, and the water in the trench. The people fell to their faces and bowed before Yahweh, the true God. Baal was exposed as an idol, and his prophets were routed.

If the modern American idol of money is to be destroyed in our lives, it will take a brave offering and the power of God himself. It will be done for you but only if you believe in God more than you care for money. And the following four steps may not only expose this modern Baal's hold on your heart; they can also rout it from your life, if you are willing.

Submit to God

As it was in Elijah's day, so it is in ours. Notice how the people who witnessed the great contest on Mount Carmel that day responded:

> When all the people saw [what had happened], they fell facedown and said, "Yahweh, He is God! Yahweh, He is God!" (1 Kings 18:39)

Dethroning the idol of mammon from your life begins with repentance and submission. It will mean bowing—literally, if necessary—and reaffirming the lordship of Jesus Christ in your life. It will mean confessing—out loud, if necessary—the ways you have pursued money and repenting of allowing it to come between you and God. It will mean reminding yourself—repeatedly, if necessary—that "Yahweh, He is God!"

I urge you to do this now. Put this book down and go to God in repentance and surrender to him your whole heart. Please don't continue until you are sure your repentance is complete.

Start Tithing

Repentance will involve more than words. It will mean literally putting your money where your mouth is and restoring God to his rightful place in your life. The Bible says, "The purpose of tithing is to teach you always to put God first in your lives" (Deut. 14:23 TLB)

If you sincerely want to overcome this idolatry toward money, then show who is truly first in your life by giving away the first 10 percent of everything you earn or inherit to God. Not because God needs the money; he doesn't. Tithing is a necessary step in breaking the stubborn grip of money on your heart and life.

If you haven't already been tithing to God, start immediately. Yes, it may be difficult. It may be painful. It may scare you. But if you cannot bring yourself to obey God in this matter, you cannot pretend that he is first in your life.

If you have already been tithing, simply continue. Tithing does not complete the process of making God first in your life any more than a cup of sugar completes the process of baking a cake. But it is a necessary ingredient.

Set Giving Goals

There's only one antidote to the modern Baal, the idol of mammon: giving. Randy Alcorn writes:

> The act of giving is a vivid reminder that it's all about God, not about us. It's saying that I am not the point. *He* is the point. He does not exist for me. I exist for Him. God's money has a higher purpose than my affluence. Giving is a joyful surrender to a greater person and a greater agenda. Giving affirms Christ's lordship. It dethrones me and exalts Him. It breaks the chains of mammon that would enslave me.[11]

If you would truly break the chains of mammon, set giving goals beyond your tithe to your local church, the community to which you belong. You might try to increase your tithe by a percent every year. You might contribute to or sponsor a special missions project of your church. You might sponsor a child in Africa, buy rice seedlings for a Cambodian family, buy a goat for a Chinese family, send Bibles to Christians in Indonesia, or send gifts to the persecuted church through Christian organizations like World Relief,[12] Partners International,[13] World Vision,[14] or Samaritan's Purse.[15] I know one family that sets a goal each year to give a portion of their giving budget anonymously, in cash, to unsuspecting people around them.

But let me also give you a warning: When you repent of the idolatry of mammon and restore God to his rightful place in your life, and go on from there to find new ways to give, it's likely to get addictive. And it's guaranteed to be rewarding because God's Word says:

> Tell those who are rich not to be proud and not to trust
> in their money, which will soon be gone. . . . Tell them
> to use their money to do good. They should . . . give
> happily to those in need, always being ready to share
> with others whatever God has given them. By doing this
> they will be storing up real treasure for themselves in
> heaven—it is the only safe investment for eternity!
> (1 Tim. 6:17–19 TLB)

Notice that he says true living comes from giving. Because, when you're giving your money away, you're storing up real treasure in heaven. A. W. Tozer wrote:

> As base a thing as money often is, it yet can be trans-
> muted into everlasting treasure. It can be converted into
> food for the hungry and clothing for the poor; it can
> keep a missionary actively winning lost men to the light
> of the gospel and thus transmute itself into heavenly
> values. Any temporal possession can be turned into ever-
> lasting wealth.[16]

Every time you tithe, every dollar you give, every act of generosity you perform, every Angel Tree gift[17] you buy, every support check you write for a campus worker or foreign missionary, you are winning a spiritual victory over mammon. With each such act, you're saying, "Yahweh, He is God!"

Stretch Yourself

> One day Jesus sat in the Temple courts with his closest friends and most devoted followers, watching worshippers come and go. As the crowds passed the Temple treasury, they would deposit their offerings into the metal collection boxes. Some givers were ostentatious. Some poured into the box streams of coins that clanged, long and loudly. But Jesus watched in silence until an old woman approached.
>
> "Watch," he said, nodding in the woman's direction.
>
> She dropped in two tiny coins so small in size and value that they barely made a sound.
>
> As she shuffled off, Jesus motioned for his disciples to lean in close to hear his words. "I assure you," he said. "This poor widow has put in more than all those giving to the temple treasury." He paused. His followers' faces showed disbelief. They all knew better . . . until he continued.
>
> "For they all gave out of their surplus, but she out of her poverty has put in everything she possessed—all she had to live on."[18]

Which characters in that account sound most like American Christians to you? Those who gave out of their surplus or the one who gave sacrificially? The answer, of course, is the former because we are far too cozy with the idol of mammon. Therefore, the best antidote is to keep giving until we are stretched.

Randy Alcorn says:

> As long as I still have something, I believe I own it. But when I give it away, I relinquish control, power, and

prestige. At the moment of release the light turns on. The magic spell is broken. My mind clears. I recognize God as owner, myself as servant, and others as intended beneficiaries of what God has entrusted to me.[19]

Richard Foster gives a memorable personal example of this in his book *Money, Sex and Power*:

> Not long ago we had a swing set, not one of those store-bought aluminum things but a real custom-made job—huge steel pipes and all. But our children would soon be beyond swing sets, so we decided that it would be good to sell it at a garage sale. My next decision was what price to put on it. I went out in the backyard and looked it over. "It should bring a good price," I thought to myself. "In fact, if I touched up the paint just a bit I could up the ante some, and if I fixed the seat on the glider I could charge even more. . . ."
>
> All of a sudden I began to monitor a spirit of covetousness within me, and I became aware of how really dangerous it was spiritually. Well, I went into the house and rather tentatively asked my wife, Carolynn, if she would mind if we gave the swing set away rather than selling it. . . . Before the day was out we had found a young couple with young children who could make good use of it, and we gave it to them—and I didn't even have to paint it! The simple act of giving crucified the greed that had gripped my heart, and the power of money was broken—for the time being.[20]

What is in your possession that can be given away? How much giving will it take to really stretch you? How soon can you transform your giving to become more like the widow Jesus commended and less like all the others who gave to the treasury that day in the temple? What, specifically, will you do immediately—today—to expose and rout the modern Baal in your heart and stretch yourself to give more than you ever thought possible?

Perhaps only God knows at this moment. But it will be exhilarating to find out.

Gracious God, I confess my flirtation with mammon. I confess that I have placed too much faith in money and far too little faith in you.

Teach me not to trust in money, which will soon be gone. Teach me to use my money to do good, to give happily to those in need, always being ready to share with others whatever you have given me. Teach me to store up real treasure for myself in heaven.

I submit to your lordship. I commit myself to a tithe. I commit to new giving goals, especially _____ and _____. And I commit to stretching myself in this "grace of giving" (2 Cor. 8:7), that I may cooperate with you in breaking the chains of mammon that would enslave me, in Jesus' name, amen.

FIFTEEN

The Martha Malady

The common clothes moth sometimes goes into a molting frenzy in its caterpillar stage. If its food intake has been insufficient, the *Tineidae* caterpillar will begin molting repeatedly, changing its skin many times, and shrinking in size with every change. "The diminution process," writes Pulitzer Prize-winning author Annie Dillard, "could, in imagination, extend to infinity, as the creature frantically shrinks and shrinks and shrinks to the size of a molecule, then an electron, but never can shrink to absolute nothing and end its terrible hunger."[1]

The clothes moth's activity is hauntingly familiar. Many of us spend our lives in similar spasms of activity. We speed through frantic work and frenzied leisure that, far from enlarging and enhancing our lives, diminishes and detracts from them. The diminution process leaves us feeling tired and stressed, always busy but never finished, always moving but never getting anywhere.

A century ago Dr. John Harvey Kellogg invented dry breakfast cereal in an effort to find a convenient and healthy alternative to the skillet full of eggs and bacon many working people enjoyed before catching the train to work. Today we eat Carnation Instant Breakfast Bars and Kellogg's Pop-Tarts for breakfast because we don't even have time for a bowl of cereal. We've trashed our percolators for instant coffeemakers with timers so we can grab a cup of coffee on the way out to the car.

Gone are the days when mom, dad, and the kids sat down for a nightly meal and swapped accounts of how their days went before spending the evening reading the newspaper, working on homework, and maybe watching *The Honeymooners* on television; today we more often grab a bite at a restaurant drive-through window before speeding to an important school or church event. Gone are the days when Mom washed and Johnny dried the dishes while chatting leisurely; today we toss the dishes into a machine so we can pile the kids into the car for Johnny's clog dancing lesson and Jessica's soccer match. Gone are the days when Mom waited for the kids to arrive home after school, ready with a snack and glasses of milk before sending them out to play while daylight lasted; today the kids may let themselves in with their own keys and occupy themselves with television or video games before Mom arrives home with a pizza for dinner.

We live in a much different world from the one in which our grandparents and parents and even we ourselves grew up. We live in a society "in which mothers work, stores don't close, assembly lines never stop, TV beckons all the time, and stock traders have to keep up with the action in Tokyo."[2] As Bill Watterson's comic-strip character Calvin tells his stuffed tiger friend, Hobbes, "The pace of modern life is all wrong. It makes every day an ordeal. Everybody's exhausted, stressed out, and short-tempered. . . . It's unnatural and unhealthy. We should *ease* into the day! You know, read the paper, have some hot cocoa, go for a leisurely walk and get our thoughts together." After Hobbes points out that such a schedule might carry into mid-afternoon, Calvin replies, "Right. Time to kick back for a little siesta and plan dinner."

It would be nice, wouldn't it? Of course. "But," we respond, "it's just not possible." We're just too busy. And it's not the culture alone that has made it so. We are busy because we choose to be busy. We are busy because we don't choose the alternative. We are busy because, for some of us, busyness has become an idol.

The Reasons for Our Busyness

We believe, of course, that we are busy for external reasons: job demands, family responsibilities, church duties, and so on. But, whether we like it or not, those external things are not the reasons for our busyness. In fact, I suspect that the reasons for such busyness are nowhere more pronounced than in the church, among those of us who follow Christ, and no less so among church leaders. Author and pastor Eugene Peterson writes:

> The one piece of mail certain to go unread into my wastebasket is the letter addressed to the "busy pastor." Not that the phrase doesn't describe me at times, but I refuse to give my attention to someone who encourages what is worst in me.
>
> I'm not arguing the accuracy of the adjective; I am, though, contesting the way it's used to flatter and express sympathy.
>
> "The poor man," we say. "He's so devoted to his flock; the work is endless, and he sacrifices himself so unstintingly." But the word *busy* is the symptom not of commitment but of betrayal. It is not devotion but defection. The adjective *busy* set as a modifier to pastor [or Christian] should sound to our ears like *adulterous* to characterize a wife or *embezzling* to describe a banker. It is an outrageous scandal, a blasphemous affront.[3]

An outrageous scandal? A blasphemous affront? Why such strong words for our busyness? Because busyness has become an idol to us. It is not a virtue. It is not a necessity. It is an idol. And we will better understand the idolatrous nature of our frantic and frenzied schedules when we confront the causes of our busyness.

Faithlessness

Many of us are busy because we don't believe God. The rest of us are busy because we don't trust God. No wonder Peterson can call our busyness a scandal and an affront to God. Because it is.

I must admit, I am preaching to myself here. God has challenged me repeatedly about the idolatry that is implicit in my busy schedule, and I continue to need reminding—and convicting—in this area. But I know that, for me at least, much of my busyness springs from my faithless heart. I honestly don't believe that God can run things without me. I don't believe that if I don't "eagerly seek all these things" (see Matt. 6:32), God will be able to pick up the pieces. In my heart of hearts, I don't believe that his timing is perfect and that if I am simply faithful today he will take care of tomorrow. I hate even to hear the words coming out of my mouth, but I don't trust him to do the things I can't—or should not—do. So I keep trying to do it all, a condition Hillary of Tours diagnosed as *irreligiosa sollicitudo pro Deo*: "a blasphemous anxiety to do God's work for him."[4]

I think that's true of many of us who are "too busy." Whether we think we're "too busy" because of our kids' countless activities or our job demands, we don't believe that saying no to some of those activities or demands is an option. Whether it's our duties to the church or the volunteer fire department that tends to fill our schedule to overflowing, we don't trust God to accomplish things in our absence, without our involvement. We fall into a "functional atheism," a mode of operation that acts—whatever we may say we believe—as if there is no power in the world besides our own.[5] We act as though we believe that God, if he happens to share our priorities and concerns, will be caught by surprise and come up short if we cease or slow our activity.

Foolishness

Another common reason for our busyness is the foolish idea that being busy makes us more important. We all know that the most important people in the world are the busiest ones, right? Well, we think so anyway. So we figure that busyness equals importance, all the while forgetting the example of Jesus, who is never depicted by the Gospel writers as being hurried or harried.

That's probably why it's often hard for me to answer the question, "How are you?" without referring to my busy schedule! We even brag to one another about how busy we are:

> "Hey, Frank, how's it going?"
> "Ah, man, I'm as busy as ever, how about you?"
> "Haven't had a day off in three months!"

Peterson exposes our busyness for the idol that it is:

> I am busy because I am vain. I want to appear important. Significant. What better way than to be busy? The incredible hours, the crowded schedule, and the heavy demands on my time are proof to myself—and to all who will notice—that I am important. . . . I live in a society in which crowded schedules and harassed conditions are evidence of importance, so I develop a crowded schedule and harassed conditions. When others notice, they acknowledge my significance, and my vanity is fed.[6]

Fecklessness

There is a third reason, it seems to me, for the busyness that so easily besets us, and that is laziness. That is, I am so constantly busy because I don't make the hard decisions and put forth the hard work to be otherwise.

To cite Eugene Peterson once more:

> I am busy because I am lazy. I indolently let others decide what I will do instead of resolutely deciding myself. I let people who do not understand the work of

the pastor [or the life of a Christ-follower] set the agenda
. . . because I am too slipshod to write it myself. . . . It
takes effort to refuse, and besides, there's always the
danger that the refusal will be interpreted as a rebuff.
    It was a favorite theme of C. S. Lewis that only lazy
people work hard. By lazily abdicating the essential work
of deciding and directing, establishing values and setting
goals, other people do it for us; then we find ourselves
frantically, at the last minute, trying to satisfy a half
dozen different demands on our time, none of which is
essential to our vocation, to stave off the disaster of
disappointing someone.[7]

Peterson is right, except that we never actually succeed in
staving off the disaster of disappointing someone; we simply
choose, consciously or not, whom we will disappoint. We disappoint God and his priorities in our lives rather than the men and
women around us. And therein lies the idolatry. We will grant the
requests and demands of hundreds of our fellow sinners while we
make God go begging. We will believe that our busyness makes us
important while telling God—the all-important One—to satisfy
himself with a subordinate place in our schedules. We will obey
everyone's demands but his and rely on our own "sufficiency"
instead of his.

It would be different if we truly believed God. It would be
different if we truly sought his glory instead of our own. It would
be different if we truly served God instead of our own ease and
comfort. It would be different. We would not be so busy. We
would not be idolaters. And we would not pay the price of our
idolatry.

The Replicas of Our Busyness

Jesus once paid a visit to the home of Mary and Martha of
Bethany. The sisters were excited and honored, of course, to have
him in their home. The sisters may have worked together to wash

his feet and those of his closest followers before ushering them all into the courtyard. I imagine the scene something like this:

> Soon after the guests arrived, Martha whispered in her sister's ear, "I'll get things started in the kitchen," and left the company of dusty, weary, hungry men to recover from the day's journey while she dashed off to prepare a meal, expecting Mary to be right behind her.
>
> But someone in the group asked Jesus a question, and when he began to answer, Mary couldn't tear herself away. Soon another question followed, and Mary sat. She lost all sense of time while the Teacher spoke, and soon she was asking him questions herself, as if she were one of his talmidim!
>
> Soon Martha was at Mary's elbow, whispering in her ear that it was time to leave the men and come help with the preparations, and Mary nodded and rose to her feet. But the Teacher still spoke, and she found it impossible to leave while those words—such words—poured from his lips. Without even realizing what she was doing, she sat again, this time closer, right at his feet.
>
> Mary absorbed every word the Teacher spoke, in spite of the increasingly loud noises her sister made in the house, until the Teacher's gaze left her own face and moved upward, and Mary turned to see Martha standing just behind her, hands on hips.
>
> Mary felt the heat of Martha's glare and opened her mouth to speak, but Martha spoke first, without moving her gaze from Mary's eyes.
>
> "Lord," Martha said, her voice strained and shrill the way it got when she was angry. "Don't you care that my sister has left me to do the work all by myself?" Her next words came out through gritted teeth. "Tell her to help me!"
>
> Mary blinked at her sister and turned to face Jesus. He wore a patient smile.
>
> "Martha," he said, waiting for her to stop glaring at her sister and look at him. "Martha, you are worried and upset about many things, but only one thing is needed."

Now it was Martha's turn to blink. She looked at
Jesus as though he spoke a foreign language.
"Mary has chosen what is better," he said, gently,
"and it will not be taken away from her."

The Results of Our Busyness

I sometimes wish Luke had not ended his account so
abruptly. I'd like to know if Mary ever got up to help Martha in
the kitchen, or if Martha served the whole group a pot of cold
porridge. I'd like to know if Martha took the bread out of the
oven and joined her sister or pouted alone in her room for the rest
of the night.

But Luke apparently knew he had said enough about that
day in Bethany. He apparently figured he had related the crucial
information. And I believe among the crucial things he reported
are indications of the price we pay for our idolatry, our exaltation
of busyness, our Martha-like obsession with "muchness and
manyness."[8]

Self-Centeredness

One of the first and most obvious results of the idol of busyness in our lives is an ungodly and unattractive focus on self.
Notice Martha's words to Jesus:

> "Lord, don't you care that *my* sister has left *me* to do the
> work *by myself*? Tell her to help *me!*" (Luke 10:40 NIV,
> emphasis added)

It's as inevitable as it is ugly, it seems. Because the roots of our
busyness are selfish, the fruit cannot be otherwise. We add more
and more to our schedule, believing that we are indispens-
able, that God and his world cannot function without our help.
Predictably, however, as our commitments increase, so does our
stress and, eventually, our resentment:

- "Can't you see I'm busy?"
- "Can't you let me have even a minute to myself?"
- "Why am I the only one who can do this right?"
- "I give and give and give, and no one seems in a hurry to help me out."
- "When do I get a little time for *me*, huh?"
- "Why do I have to do the work *by myself?* Tell her to *help me!*"

It's all about me. My schedule. My calendar. My to-do list. My pressures. My importance. My indispensability. It's all about me because I am the busy one. I am the martyr. I am at the center of the storm.

Separation from God

It is easy to sympathize with Martha. She was doing the work. She was the responsible one. She was thinking ahead, planning, preparing. Who can fault her?

But the fact is, the King of Glory paid Martha a visit, and she sat him down and hurried off into the next room. She had the Bread of Life in her home, and she was in the kitchen rolling bread dough. The Desire of the Nations had shown up on her doorstep, and she turned her thoughts to what everyone might want for dinner.

But then, we are no different in our exaltation of busyness. We choose crowded calendars over communion with God. Day after day, week after week, and month after month goes by while our distance from God increases. Every moment we spend worshipping at the altar of busyness is time we neglect to spend at Jesus' feet. Not that we would use all our time for the worship of God. Not at all. But inasmuch as our busyness is an idol, it will inevitably separate us from God.

This may help to explain why so many "busy pastors" and other busy people in ministry become bitter and cynical as they give more and more in "God's service." They are striving—whether faithlessly, foolishly, or fecklessly, it doesn't much matter—but they are not serving God; they are serving an idol. They are not growing closer to God but more distant.

Mary, on the other hand, chose the one thing that really matters in life: communion with God. Jesus' presence was more important to her than any preparations. She apparently believed that time with him was the ideal use of her time, not idle time. She clearly knew Jesus desired her company more than her cooking. She chose the "one thing" all of us need:

> One thing I ask of the Lord,
>   this is what I seek:
> that I may dwell in the house of the Lord
>   all the days of my life,
> to gaze upon the beauty of the Lord
>   and to seek him in his temple.
> For in the day of trouble,
>   he will keep me . . .
>   he will hide me . . .
>   and set me high upon a rock. (Ps. 27:4–5 NIV)

Sacrifice of "Better Things"

Martha's busyness distracted her and drew her away from Jesus. And Jesus pointed out the contrast between Mary's choice and Martha's choice: "Mary has chosen what is better, and it will not be taken away from her" (Luke 10:42 NIV).

Just before saying that, Jesus had emphasized to Martha that Mary had chosen the "one thing" that was crucial and necessary. But here he talks of "what is better." Perhaps we may infer something from that: there are "better things" that result from Mary's kind of lifestyle than from Martha's. Busyness cheats us of those "better things." When we pursue frantic and frenzied lifestyles, we like Martha will experience the loss of "better things."

We lose a sense of peace. Our lives are so crammed with activity that when we do manage a few moments of quiet, they are characterized more by stupor than by serenity. "Sometimes I sits and thinks," said the hillbilly, "and sometimes I just sits." But we have forgotten how to do either. We no longer sit, and we no longer think; inaction is as foreign to us as contemplation. Some of us even try listening to motivational and educational tapes *while we sleep!* Yet our efforts to pack in so much of what we want into our lives manage to crowd out so much of what we need: relaxation, re-creation, serenity, tranquility—in a word, peace.

We lose a sense of pace. Life at its best possesses a rhythm, a kind of pace, a rotation like the seasons the Creator so wisely and beautifully built into nature. Like the lives of animals that mate in the spring, raise young in the summer, scamper about and store food in the autumn, and hibernate through the winter, human life is designed to possess a certain pace. But we have lost the recreative and restorative pace of sowing and reaping, waking and sleeping, workweek and Sabbath. Our summers are much like our winters. Our weekends are much like our weeks. Our lives at home are as harried as our lives at work. The hills and valleys that once formed the landscapes of our lives have flattened into an endless, monotonous interstate highway on which the only object is to drive as fast as possible.

We lose a sense of place. When is the last time you enjoyed the scenery on your drive to work or church? When is the last time you really looked at the sky? When did you last spend time in front of your fireplace, watching the shadows cast on the wall by the flames? When did your neighbors last see you for more than thirty seconds? Such moments are not only the stuff of English novels; they also impart a sense of place to us. They foster a feeling of belonging, an atmosphere of security. They are like refuges in the landscapes of our lives, safe havens where—no matter how far or fast we may travel—we know we can find a home. Our frantic lives, however, can leave us feeling like aliens in our own communities, like visitors in our own homes.

Most of us recognize, of course, that we are missing much as a result of the pace and pressure of modern life, but we feel helpless to *do* anything about it. It would be nice to sit at Jesus' feet, make him our focus, even have a cup of cocoa or go for a leisurely walk, but we *can't*. We think hectic and harried lives are not only *normal* these days; we also believe they are *necessary*. We agree it would be preferable to be like Mary, but we don't really believe it's possible.

But it is. And it's not only possible but critical. Our busyness may be a stubborn idol, but it is an idol, nonetheless, and one we must destroy before it destroys us.

The Reversal of Our Busyness

For most of us, our busyness has deep roots, and it developed over time. For some of us, it may be the sort of spiritual challenge that requires extreme measures (Mark 9:29).

Roughly twenty-five hundred years ago, a prophet named Haggai delivered a message from God that still seems to apply to our busy lives today. He said:

> Now this is what the LORD Almighty says: "Give careful thought to your ways. You have planted much, but have harvested little. You eat, but never have enough. You drink, but never have your fill. You put on clothes, but are not warm. You earn wages, only to put them in a purse with holes in it. . . . You expected much, but see, it turned out to be little. What you brought home, I blew away. Why?" declares the LORD Almighty. "Because of my house, which remains a ruin, *while each of you is busy with his own* house." (Hag. 1:5–6, 9 NIV, emphasis added)

The repentant heart will respond to the idol of busyness by giving careful thought to its ways, seeking God in prayer, and asking him to shine his searchlight into its corners and crevasses. Have you been neglecting God while you've been keeping busy with your own "stuff"? Have you been planting, eating, drinking, earning with little to show for it all? Have you been acting as though it all depends on you instead of depending on God for it all?

These are not easy questions to answer, I know. And even when they are answered, they are not easy to correct. So I'm going to prescribe perhaps the hardest spiritual exercise of all: a "busyness fast."

Now, don't panic. You can take it a step at a time. But if busyness has become an idol in your life, it will not come out except by prayer and fasting; I strongly urge you, in the name of Jesus, to be willing to take extreme measures in the interest of extreme improvement.

To begin, fast from "busyness" one day. Cancel all prior engagements. Say no to new appointments. Use the day for work or pleasure, but make sure to include ample time to sit at Jesus' feet and spend time in prayer and meditation.

Expand your one-day fast to three days. Block out a three-day period in the next month when you will accept no prescheduled meetings, appointments, or engagements.

Establish a weekly Sabbath. Keep at least one day a week free from appointments, commitments, and obligations, a day unlike the other six. No work, no agenda, nothing to remember. A day to focus on God in a special way. A day to slow down, take inventory, and be spontaneous. My Sabbath typically includes four activities: prayer, reading, walking, and napping. I leave the television, radio, and CD player off. I try not to drive anywhere if I can help it. And I don't answer the phone. It's amazing that the world survives without me for those twenty-four hours, but it does. (If you need more help and motivation to begin, read Marva Dawn's excellent book *Keeping the Sabbath Wholly*).

Use your weekly Sabbath to define your workweek, not the other way around. If you can cease from the idolatry of busyness one day a week on a regular basis, you can—with God's help—cast down the idol of busyness even in the midst of your workweek. You can begin to let the spirit of the Sabbath—the spirit of trust in God, not your own ability or activity—infect the other days of the week. Ask God to cast from your heart any spirit of faithlessness, foolishness, or fecklessness and install faith in him in its place.

There can be deliverance from the idol of busyness. There can be release from frantic work and frenzied leisure. There can be relief from being always busy but never finished, always moving but never getting anywhere.

> *Father, thank you for revealing to me the danger of busyness in my life. I don't want to be faithless, foolish, or feckless. Please show me the extent of my own tendencies to bow to the idol of busyness. Convince and convict me of all ungodliness. I repent; help me to bear fruit in keeping with repentance (see Luke 3:8).*
>
> *Help me truly and wholeheartedly to believe in you and not in myself, my abilities, or my activity. Help me to find significance in you and in my obedience to you, not in the false importance of busyness. Help me to overcome the laziness of letting other people set my schedule for me and not lazily abdicate the essential work of deciding and directing, establishing values, and setting goals.*
>
> *Finally, Lord, teach me the bane of busyness in my life and the hurt that hurry does to me, and bless my earliest efforts at overcoming this idol with early rewards that I might sit at your feet and learn to enjoy the "better things" that come only—and generously—from you, in Jesus' name, amen.*

Afterword

by Matt Metzger
(*American Idols* veteran
and *One Life to Live* television star)

I felt like an injured gladiator on the floor of the Coliseum awaiting his fate. Exhausted from having given my all, I stood there smiling uneasily. All eyes were on me: cameras, lights, microphones focused on capturing my reaction and broadcasting it to the world. Thumbs-up or thumbs-down? I was completely at the mercy of the infamous trio: Randy, Paula, and Simon. After an unnecessarily dramatic deliberation (obviously designed to make me sweat profusely), two of the three thumbs pointed upwards, and I received my yellow paper with those enticing words: "You're going to Hollywood!" And so began my quest to become the next American Idol.

As the coming months rolled by, I found myself miraculously progressing through the rounds of auditions and into the first group of eight contestants from *American Idol* season 3's top 32. Nervous, I stumbled my way through Marc Cohn's hit, "Walking in Memphis," which earned me national television exposure, third place in my group, and a one-way ticket home because only the top two in the group advanced that day.

Weeks later, however, I was given another chance when I was invited back for the "wild card" round. I chose to sing "When I See You Smile," the Bad English song. But despite the second chance and my best effort, that performance ended my quest to become an American Idol.

That night, as I stood in my hotel bathroom, rehashing the day's events, tears began to well up in my eyes. I quickly wiped them away and wondered what was going on. Sure, I was disappointed that I hadn't performed as well as I had hoped, but I told myself I shouldn't be crying. I trusted God with my life. I knew he had a plan. So why the tears?

I lay down on my hotel bed in the darkened room, stared at the ceiling, and realized where the streaks on my face came from. I was terrified. The rug had been pulled out from underneath me, and I had no idea what to do. My wedding was six months away, and I had no job, no money, and no plan.

Just the day before I had it all figured out. *American Idol* was my ticket to providing for my (soon-to-be) wife and (eventual) family, becoming a celebrity, and serving God through my newfound wealth and influence. But, like seventy-five thousand others that year, my *American Idol* dream ended only in disappointment. I had staked everything on that dream. I had built my plans and expectations on it. It had become my focus, what I sought after. I may have had good intentions, but the life that *American Idol* offered had itself become an idol to me.

In Greek mythology, the Sirens were creatures who sang alluring songs to lure sailors to shipwreck along rocky coasts where they would be destroyed. That's what idols do. They entice you with alluring, even irresistible, promises and then leave you empty-handed, perhaps even shipwrecked and destroyed.

I hope that's not your experience. I pray this book has found you in time. I trust you will heed its warnings and "flee from idolatry" (1 Cor. 10:14).

I discovered how easy it is to stop focusing on God and his plans and turn to an idol. But when I finally recognized my idolatry and repented from it, God met me there, purified my heart again, and gave me a single-minded devotion once more. And in the months that followed, he brought me and my bride to New York, where I've been working as an actor, living the adventure he has planned for my life, instead of some cheap imitation I dreamed up on my own. Sometimes I wonder how I could have ever considered settling for anything less.

I don't suppose I've waged my last battle against idolatry. I imagine I'll have to be vigilant if I'm going to put my trust in God and not the things of this world and the prolific, pervasive idols of the culture I live and work in. But I hope I'll always remember this: the moment I was ready to expel my idol from the throne of my life, God was ready to take his rightful place as King of my heart. I know he will do the same for you.

> *Jesus calls us from the worship*
> *Of the vain world's golden store,*
> *From each idol that would keep us,*
> *Saying, "Christian, love Me more."*

> *In our joys and in our sorrows,*
> *Days of toll and hours of ease,*
> *Still He calls, in cares and pleasures,*
> *"Christian, love Me more than these."*
> —Cecil Francis Alexander

How to Find the Church That's Right for You

Maybe you've just moved into a new community. Maybe your church closed. Maybe you're at a new stage in life. Maybe you're a new Christ follower. Or maybe you've only recently decided to obey God in committing yourself to a local church community. There may be many reasons you're looking for a church. But you are.

If you're trying to find a new church, for whatever reason, you're in a precarious position. There are many poor reasons to choose a church but only a few good ones, particularly when measured against what Luke, the author of Acts, considered important enough to mention as characteristics of the First Church of Jerusalem.

1. Is it biblical?

Acts 2:42 says, "They devoted themselves to the apostles' teaching" (Acts 2:42 NIV).

In other words the First Church of Jerusalem was devoted to learning God's Word from the apostles; they applied themselves to solid Bible teaching. So a fundamental thing to ascertain about any church is what they teach. Look closely at their statement of faith. Don't join a church without investigating whether they truly believe and effectively teach the Bible.

2. Will it help me connect with others?

Acts 2:42 also says of the early church: "They devoted themselves to the apostles' teaching and to the fellowship (Acts 2:42 NIV).

In other words, they were devoted to one another, to relationships, to being part of the family of God. So look at the church and ask, is this a place where I can develop relationships with others? Can this church help me obey the Bible's commands to . . .

> have fellowship with one another
> greet one another
> love one another
> accept one another
> be devoted
> be kind and compassionate to one another.
> (1 John 1:7; Rom. 16:16; John 13:35; Rom. 15:7,
> 12:10; Eph. 4:32)

Do people just file out after an hour of worship and get into their cars? Or do they stick around and pray or laugh or cry together? Is this a place where I can feel part of a family? Are there small groups I can be a part of? Lunches? Picnics?

3. Does it help me connect with God?

Acts 2:42 further says that the early church "devoted themselves . . . to the breaking of bread" (Acts 2:42 NIV).

Now, it's not obvious to us as it would have been to first-century readers, but that's talking about the worship of the church. They met in homes to celebrate Communion, a symbolic ceremony commemorating Jesus' sacrifice on the cross; that was the centerpiece of their weekly worship. So it's also important to ask, "Does this church's worship style help me connect with God?"

Because we're all different, different ways of worshipping will speak to our hearts in different ways. The Bible doesn't say, "Thou shalt use pipe organs; guitars are an abomination to the Lord." Neither does it say, "Take heed that you stand when everybody else stands, lest God be angry with you." No, the Bible says, "Those who worship [God] must worship [Him] in spirit and in truth" (John 4:24 NLT).

If you're worshipping in spirit and truth, God doesn't care two bits about the style, whether it's formal or casual, traditional or contemporary, loud or quiet, reflective or emotional. The question is, does it connect you with God?

4. Is it a praying church?

Acts 2:42 also says that the First Church of Jerusalem "devoted themselves . . . to prayer" (NIV).

People don't often ask this question when they're looking at a church, but Luke clearly thought it was important enough to mention. The early church was devoted to prayer.

If it is true, as author E. M. Bounds has said, that "God does nothing but in answer to prayer," then if you want to find a church where something is happening, where God is moving, where you're going to be glad you stuck around, look for a praying church. Whatever else may be missing in that church, it won't be missing for long if it's a praying church.

5. Do I see people being changed?

The next verse in the second chapter of Acts says, "Everyone was filled with awe, and many wonders and miraculous signs were done by the apostles" (2:43 NIV).

The people in this Jerusalem church of the first century were not the same people they'd always been. They were being healed.

They were growing spiritually. They were becoming servants. Some were becoming leaders.

God wants the same for you. He wants you to grow, change, become mature. The purpose of a good church is to help you grow spiritually and to develop spiritual maturity. So look around. Are people being changed? Are they showing signs of growth? Are there "God at work" signs around the place?

6. Is it characterized by unity?

Acts 2:44 says, "All the believers were together and had everything in common" (NIV). They "were together." There weren't divisions in the church. And keep in mind, this was *the* church in Jerusalem. Not just the folks who got along with one another or the folks who lifted their hands when they sang. This was *everybody*. All kinds. They were all together and had everything in common.

So look at the church and ask, "Are there factions or parties in the church? Is there an 'us/them' attitude toward other churches? Or are they characterized by a spirit of unity?"

7. Is it a giving church?

Acts 2:45 says, "Selling their possessions and goods, they gave to anyone as he had need" (NIV).

It is so easy as a church to get inwardly focused and concentrate on budgets and expenses until we give people the impression that we're only after their money. In fact, many people say their impression of the church is that "all they want is my money."

But notice: The First Church of Jerusalem wasn't raking in the dough; they were cranking out the dough! They were giving stuff away! They gave to "*any*one as he had need."

Apparently they actually *believed* Jesus' words that "it is more blessed to give than to receive" (Acts 20:35 NIV). That's the kind of church you want to be a part of, a giving church, a church that's not hoarding but meeting people's needs in and outside of the church.

8. Is there a place for me to serve?

Acts 2:46 starts by saying, "Every day they continued to meet together in the temple courts. They broke bread in their homes and ate together with glad and sincere hearts, praising God. . . ." (NIV).

Everyone in the church played a part, an active role. It took teachers, cooks, hosts, worship leaders, all kinds of servants to make the church go.

The "they" of verses 46 and 47 is everybody. It wasn't just the men, just the "insiders," just those with degrees. It was "they." Everyone.

This is important, yet it's probably the most overlooked thing to look for in finding the church that's best for you. People ask, "Do you have a children's program?" or "Do you have a singles ministry?" Or "a women's group" or a "men's group"?

I don't think I've *ever* been asked by a person checking out a church, "Do you need Bible study leaders? Could I offer my baking skills to this church? Are there ways I can serve?" But that is a biblical and Christlike attitude.

The Bible says, "There are different kinds of service . . . and together you form the Body of Christ and each one of you is *a necessary part* of it" (see 1 Cor. 12:5, 27 TLB, italics added).

If you're a Christ follower and you don't fit into your place and do what God made you to do, serve as God made you to serve, a *necessary* part is missing from the body.

9. Is it making an impact in the community?

The latter part of verse 47 says the Jerusalem church was "enjoying the favor of all the people" (Acts 2:47 NIV). This church was enjoying the favor not only of those *in* the church, but of "*all* the people." It was having an impact in the community. People were taking notice of these Christ followers. They were winning the respect of outsiders.

There will always be people who can find fault with the church, and we should always please God first, not men; but it's a fair question to ask if the church is having any impact in the community. Is it a credit to the gospel of Jesus Christ? Is it making a difference, earning respect?

10. Will it help me accomplish my mission?

Notice Acts 2:47: "And the Lord added to their number daily those who were being saved" (NIV). This church was clearly reaching out to others, fulfilling the mission that had been given them by Jesus:

> Go and make disciples of all nations, baptizing them in the name of the Father and of the Son and of the Holy Spirit, and teaching them to obey everything I have commanded you. (Matt. 28:19–20 NIV)

If you want to find the church that's best for you, look for one that helps you fulfill your mission, that helps you reach out to others and introduce them to the joy of knowing God and following Jesus Christ.

Of course, there's no such thing as a perfect church. And all will be stronger in some areas than in others on the above list. But if you use the same criteria in finding the church that's best for you that Luke used in describing the first-century church in Jerusalem, you'll likely make a much better choice for yourself and for the kingdom of God.

Notes

Foreword

1. Bill Hybels, *Laws That Liberate* (Wheaton, Ill.: Victor Books, 1985), 10.

Chapter 1

1. Elyse Fitzpatrick, *Idols of the Heart* (Phillipsburg, N.J.: P&R Publishing, 2001), 13–14.
2. Marshall Allen, "American Idols IV: Ditching the Idols," *Boundless Webzine,* May 2004.
3. Fitzpatrick, *Idols of the Heart,* 65.
4. Ibid., 110.
5. John Calvin, *Institutes of the Christian Religion,* vol. 1, John T. McNeill, ed. (Philadelphia, Pa.: Westminster, 1960), 108.
6. Oswald Chambers, *My Utmost for His Highest* (updated edition), James Reimann, ed. (Grand Rapids, Mich.: Discovery House, 1992), April 3.
7. Allen, "American Idols IV: Ditching the Idols."

Chapter 2

1. Jon Swartz, "Some eBay Sellers Are Going, Going, Gone," *USA Today,* 2 February 2005, 3B.

2. Marshall Allen, "American Idols II: The Pursuit of Happiness," *Boundless Webzine,* May 2004.

3. Herbert Schlossberg, *Idols for Destruction* (Wheaton, Ill.: Crossway Books, 1990), 107.

4. Allen, "American Idols II: The Pursuit of Happiness."

5. Ibid.

6. James Dobson, *What Wives Wish Their Husbands Knew About Women* (Wheaton, Ill.: Tyndale House Publishers, 1979), 108.

Chapter 3

1. William Steig, *Yellow and Pink* (New York: Farrar, Straus and Giroux, 2003).

2. Carl Sagan, *Cosmos* (New York: Ballantine Books, 1985), 1.

3. H. Thomas and D. L. Thomas, *Living Biographies of Great Philosophers* (New York: Blue Ribbon Books, 1941), 44.

4. The seventeenth-century mathematician, philosopher, and author of the book, *Pensees* (Thoughts).

5. Humanitarian doctor and coauthor (with Philip Yancey) of the book *Fearfully and Wonderfully Made* (Grand Rapids, Mich.: Zondervan, 1997).

6. William Shakespeare, *Hamlet,* act I, scene v, line 166.

7. Cited by Charles W. Colson (with Nancy Pearcey) in *How Now Shall We Live?* (Wheaton, Ill.: Tyndale House Publishers, 1999), 91.

8. Colson with Pearcey, *How Now Shall We Live?,* 94–95.

9. David Duncan, *Life and Letters of Herbert Spencer* (London: Methuen Publishers, 1908), 319.

10. Thomas Henry Huxley, *Life and Letters of Thomas Henry Huxley* (New York: D. Appleton and Company, 1909), 246.

11. Richard Lewontin, "Billions and Billions of Demons," *New York Review of Books,* 9 January 1997, 31.

12. William Darwin, quoted in John Durant, *Darwinism and Divinity* (Oxford and New York: Basil Blackwell, 1985), 38.

13. Herbert Schlossberg, *Idols for Destruction* (Wheaton, Ill.: Crossway Books, 1990), 144–45.

14. William B. Provine and Phillip E. Johnson, "Darwinism: Science or Naturalistic Philosophy?" (videotape of debate held at Stanford University, 30 April 1994). Available from Access Research Network, P.O. Box 38069, Colorado Springs, CO 80937–8069.

15. Ingrid Newkirk, cofounder of People for the Ethical Treatment of Animals (PETA) famously told *Vogue* magazine in 1989, "A rat is a pig is a dog is a boy. They are all mammals."

Chapter 4

1. Robinson Jeffers, "Shine, Republic," *Selected Poems* (New York: Vintage Books, 1965), 57.

2. Don Closson, "The Empty Self," Probe Ministries (www.leaderu.com/orgs/probe/docs/emptyself.html).

3. Ralph C. Wood, "Baylor Reaps the Enlightenment Whirlwind," *Christianity Today,* 7 October 2003 (www.christianity today.com/ct/2003/140/21.0.html).

4. Doug Wilson, "Individualism," *Credenda Agenda,* vol. 14, Issue 3 (www.credenda.org/issues/14-3presbyterion.php?type= print).

5. Ibid.

6. John Donne, *Devotions Upon Emergent Occasions,* Meditation XVII.

7. Wood, "Baylor Reaps the Enlightenment Whirlwind."

8. Howard G. Hendricks, "A Mandate for Mentoring," in Jack Hayford, *Seven Promises of a Promise Keeper* (Nashville: W Publishing Group, 1999), 37.

9. Ibid., 38.

10. Ibid., 39.

Chapter 5

1. Tony Evans, *Who Is This King of Glory?* (Chicago: Moody Press, 1999), introduction.

2. Daniel Boorstin, *The Image: A Guide to Pseudo-Events in America* (New York: Vintage, 1992), 57ff.

3. Maria Puente, "The Sweet Smell of Excess," *USA Today,* 23 February 2005 (www.usatoday.com/life/people/2005-02-03-celeb-auctions_x.htm?POE=LIFISVA).

4. Marva Dawn, *Reaching Out without Dumbing Down* (Grand Rapids, Mich.: Wm. B. Eerdmans Publishing Company, 1995), 50–51.

5. Puente, "The Sweet Smell of Excess."

6. Keturah Gray, "Celebrity Worship Syndrome: Is America's Obsession with Stardom Becoming Unhealthy?" (http://abc news.go.com/sections/entertainment/Living/celebrityworship 030923.html).

Chapter 6

1. Comment on a Web site tribute to Now and Laters (www.old timecandy.com/now-later.htm).

2. Barry Farber, "Natural-Born Sellers," *Entrepreneur Magazine,* May 2004 (www.entrepreneur.com/article/0,4621,315178,00.html).

3. Roy Rivenburg, "Our Instant Gratification Culture Often Makes It Tough to Resist Temptation," *The Seattle Times,* 20 April 2004.

4. See Matthew 4:1–11.

5. Roy Rivenburg, "Our Instant Gratification Culture."

Chapter 7

1. Michael Gove, "We Should Fear the Disturbing Future Where Man Becomes Superman," *The London Times,* 12 October 2004 (www.timesonline.co.uk/article/0,8122-1305837,00.html).

2. Josh McDowell and Bob Hostetler, *Right from Wrong* (Dallas: Word Publishing, 1994), 29–30.

3. Erich Fromm, *Beyond the Chains of Illusions* (New York: Simon and Schuster, 1962), 174–82.

4. Ray Stedman, "Controlling God," 1968, copyright Discovery Publishing, a ministry of Peninsula Bible Church (http://pbc. org/dp/stedman/genesis/0332.html%20&SermonID=542).

5. "The Humanist Manifesto," copyright 1973 by the American Humanist Association (www.americanhumanist.org/about/mani festo1.html).

6. John Lennon, "Imagine," copyright 1972 by EMI Blackwood Music/Lenono Music.

7. Stedman, "Controlling God."

8. "The Humanist Manifesto II," copyright 1973 by the American Humanist Association (www.americanhumanist.org/ about/manifesto2.html).

9. Stedman, "Controlling God."

10. Ibid.

Chapter 8

1. *The Works of Jonathan Edwards* (Edinburgh: Banner of Truth, 1984), 6:27ff.

2. Lloyd J. Ogilvie, *The Communicator's Commentary*, vol. 5: Acts (Waco, Tex.: Word Books, 1983), 158.

3. John Ortberg and Pam Howell, "Can You Engage Both Heart and Mind?" *Leadership Journal*, Spring 1999.

4. Marva Dawn, *Reaching Out without Dumbing Down* (Grand Rapids, Mich.: Wm. B. Eerdmans Publishing Company, 1995), 77.

5. E. Stanley Jones, *The Way to Power and Poise* (New York: Abingdon-Cokesbury Press, 1949), 13.

6. Matthew Henry, *Commentary on the Whole Bible* (Grand Rapids, Mich.: Zondervan Publishing Company, 1961), 1666.

7. Ogilvie, *The Communicator's Commentary*, 158.

8. Ibid., 158–59.

9. Oswald Chambers, *My Utmost for His Highest* (Updated Edition), James Reimann, ed. (Grand Rapids, Mich.: Discovery House, 1992), December 21.

Chapter 9

1. Marshall Allen, "American Idols III: The American Dream," *Boundless Webzine*, May 2004.

2. Ibid.

3. Ibid.

4. Tony Campolo, *The Success Fantasy* (Wheaton, Ill.: Victor Books, 1980), 19.

5. Ibid., 15–16.

6. Jim Kallam, *Risking Church* (Colorado Springs, Colo.: Waterbrook Press, 2003), 52.

7. Campolo, *The Success Fantasy*, 16.

8. Richard Foster, *Money, Sex and Power* (San Francisco, Calif.: Harper & Row, 1985), 228.

9. Michael Korda, *Success* (New York: Random House, 1977), 4.

10. Foster, *Money, Sex and Power*, 231.

11. Phrasing borrowed from Brennan Manning, *Abba's Child* (Colorado Springs, Colo.: NavPress, 1994), 84.

Chapter 10

1. "The Boobs Tube," *American Enterprise*, April 2001 (© 2001, American Enterprise Institute for Public Policy Research), (www.find articles.com/p/articles/mi_m2185/is_3_12/ai_72611037).

2. Irving Kristol, "Sex, Violence and Videotape," *Wall Street Journal*, 31 May 1994.

3. Jerome Weeks, "Sex Moves from Back Shelf to Bookstores' Front Tables," *The Dallas Morning News*, 26 January 2005 (www.azcentral.com/ent/arts/articles/0126sexbooks26.html).

4. Philip Yancey, "Holy Sex," *Christianity Today*, October 2003 (www.christianitytoday.com/ct/2003/010/3.46.html).

5. According to an August 2000 *Christianity Today* survey (www.thencsp.com/pornfacts.htm).

6. Stephen Arterburn and Fred Stoeker with Mike Yorkey, *Every Man's Battle* (Colorado Springs, Colo.: Waterbrook Press, 2000), 25–26.

7. Foster, *Money, Sex and Power*, 95.

8. Ibid.

9. Ibid.

10. Ibid.

11. Ibid., 96–97.

12. Ibid., 97.

13. Ibid.

14. Arterburn and Stoeker, *Every Man's Battle*, 28.

15. Foster, *Money, Sex and Power*, 99.

16. Steve Gallagher, *At the Altar of Sexual Idolatry* (Dry Ridge, Ky.: Pure Life Ministries, 2000), 74–75.

17. Ibid., 76–77.

Chapter 11

1. Web slogan from the XM Satellite Radio Web site (www.xm radio.com).

2. "Choose the Sex of Your Baby," 11 August 2004, *60 Minutes II* (www.cbsnews.com/stories/2004/04/13/60II/main611618.shtml).

3. See Mary McNamara, "Era of the Gender Crosser," *Los Angeles Times*, 26 February 2001, available on the Web site of the National Transgender Advocacy Coalition (www.ntac.org/news/01/03/10 era.html).

4. Cited by Mark Bergin in "Rogue State," *World Magazine,* 9 April 2005, 23.

5. William J. Doherty, quoted by Mark Wolf in "Staying afloat: How to resist the urge to jump ship," *Rocky Mountain News,* 14 July 2001.

6. Randy Alcorn's story is one of God's ability to take what is evil and turn it to good; see Alcorn's book, *The Treasure Principle* (Sisters, Ore.: Multnomah Press, 2001).

7. Marshall Allen, "American Idols: Free to Be Me," *Boundless Webzine,* May 2004.

8. Ibid.

Chapter 12

1. Marshall Allen, "American Idols: Free to Be Me," *Boundless Webzine,* May 2004.

2. Walter Wangerin, *The Book of God* (Grand Rapids, Mich.: Zondervan, 1996), 418–21.

3. C. F. Keil, *Commentary on the Old Testament,* vol. 3 (Grand Rapids, Mich.: Wm. B. Eerdmans Publishing Company, 1983), 345.

4. William Barclay, *The Daily Study Bible: The Letters to Timothy, Titus, and Philemon,* rev. ed. (Philadelphia, Pa.: Westminster Press, 1975), 66.

Chapter 13

1. Adapted from www.interstel.net/~jdpaul/stupidity.wilderness.comments.html.

2. Robert Wuthnow, "Small Groups Forge Notions . . . of the Sacred," *Christian Century,* 8 December 1993, 1239–40.

Chapter 14

1. Richard Foster, *Money, Sex and Power* (San Francisco, Calif.: Harper & Row, 1985), 26.

2. Mark Twain, "Concerning the Jews," *Harper's Magazine,* March 1898.

3. The quotes in this account are taken directly from the Holman Christian Standard Bible®, Mark 10:17–21.

4. Gordon MacDonald, *Secrets of the Generous Life* (Wheaton, Ill.: Tyndale House Publishers, 2002), 95.

5. Foster, *Money, Sex and Power,* 27.

6. Dietrich Bonhoeffer, *The Cost of Discipleship* (New York: Macmillan Publishing Company, 1963), 196.

7. Thomas J. Stanley and William D. Danko, *The Millionaire Next Door* (New York: Pocket Books, 1998).

8. Foster, *Money, Sex and Power,* 24–25.

9. Joyce Meyer, quoted in "The Prosperity Gospel," by Bill Smith and Carolyn Tuft, *St. Louis Post-Dispatch,* 18 November 2003.

10. Foster, *Money, Sex and Power,* 56.

11. Randy Alcorn, *The Treasure Principle* (Sisters, Ore.: Multnomah Publishers, 2001), 57.

12. See www.wr.org.

13. See www.partnersintl.org.

14. See www.worldvisiongifts.org.

15. See www.samaritan.org.

16. A. W. Tozer, *Born after Midnight* (Harrisburg, Pa.: Christian Publications, 1959), 107.

17. See www.pfm.org/AM/Template.cfm?Section=Angel_Tree1.

18. The quotes in the last two paragraphs of this account are taken directly from the Holman Christian Standard Bible®, Mark 12:43–44.

19. Randy Alcorn, *The Treasure Principle,* 57.

20. Richard Foster, *Money, Sex and Power,* 61–62.

Chapter 15

1. Annie Dillard, *Pilgrim at Tinker Creek* (San Francisco, Calif.: HarperPerennial, 1974), 171.

2. Anastasia Toufexis, in "Drowsy America," *Time,* 17 December 1990, 78.

3. Eugene Peterson, *The Contemplative Pastor* (Grand Rapids, Mich.: Wm. B. Eerdmans Publishing Co., 1989), 17.

4. Ibid., 17–18.

5. Parker Palmer, *Leading from Within* (Washington, D.C.: Servant Leadership School, 1990), 16.

6. Peterson, *The Contemplative Pastor,* 18.

7. Ibid., 18–19.

8. Richard Foster, *Prayer: Finding the Heart's True Home* (San Francisco, Calif.: HarperSanFrancisco, 1992), 1.